Release T

Three Philosophic Dialogues

*Being a tribute to, and a celebration of, Socrates,
Plato and the golden Platonic Tradition*

"Where the desire of any soul is, and such as is its condition, there each
of us nearly resides, and such for the most part each of us subsists."
The Laws 904c

Guy Wyndham-Jones

The Prometheus Trust

The Prometheus Trust
28 Petticoat Lane
Dilton Marsh
Westbury
Wiltshire
BA13 4DG

Release Thyself
Three Philosophic Dialogues

Guy Wyndham-Jones

Copyright 2011

ISBN 978 1 898910 565

The Prometheus Trust is a registered
UK Charity, number 299648

Guy Wyndham-Jones asserts
the moral right to be identified as
the author of this book.

British Library Catalogue-in-Publication Data
A catalogue record for this book is
available from the British Library.

Printed and bound in the UK by the
MPG Books Group, Bodmin and King's Lynn

Contents

Preface i

Introduction..iii

The Dialogues

    The Therapon 1

    The Alphaeus 45

    The Platon 95

Fruits

    To Niké.. 134

    Our Loss 135

    The Voice of Wisdom............................ 136

    Golden Chain 137

    On facing the Morning Sun.................... 138

    To Mother Earth 139

    Life.. 140

    The Heart of Love.............................. 141

    To Beauty....................................... 142

    Upon reading Sacred Works 143

    To Socrates 144

    Children of the Sea............................ 145

    To Plato 146

Dedicated to all lovers of wisdom
and friends of truth,
everywhere . . .

Εισι παντα πυρος ενος εκγεγαωτα

Preface

The works of great men and women serve to call us lesser mortals to the contemplation of profound ideas and beautiful ideals as well as allowing us a clearer vision of our place in the divine universe: they are inspiring and life-enhancing. However, their very power often means that other creative individuals feel unable to place their own endeavours too close to such masterpieces of human geniuses: what playwright, for example, would dare attempt a second Hamlet? Just as a well-established tree's spread of branches tends to prevent the growth of saplings within its shade, so the best of human art throws a creative shadow across its near ground. The dialogues of Plato – full of goodness, wisdom and beauty as they are – may most certainly be counted amongst these mighty works.

For this reason, the author of these three philosophical dialogues (centred around the imagined conversations of Socrates and his associates) has approached his task with some trepidation – certain in the knowledge that in any comparison between these and the dialogues of Plato, his own will come a distant second. So why write them? The answer, I think, lies in one of the fundamental drives of human nature, or indeed, if we are to believe the discourse of Diotima in the *Symposium*, the fundamental drive of all creatures: that of love. Love, above all things, allows us to overcome our fears – it leads us from our familiar world in which we seem to be both safe and comfortable into one full of unknown possibilities. I have known Guy Wyndham-Jones throughout the forty years of my adult life, and have never doubted that his love of the wisdom that lies at the heart of the Platonic tradition is the power which has drawn him ever onwards, leading him to ignore the safe options of life, and pursue the best.

A life lived in this way, of course, will know failures: read any fairy story, and its hero or heroine is likely to encounter setback after setback, and sometimes be brought to the very brink of death – but the quest is considered worth even this. In truth, we should see the purpose of these quests not as the gaining of the stated prize, but the unfolding of the real nature of the hero: in the words of Socrates (in the *Phaedrus*), "To endeavour after beautiful attainments is beautiful, as likewise to endure whatever may happen to be the result of our endeavours."

These dialogues are, then, an endeavour after beautiful attainments.

ii *Release Thyself*

A tradition is not something to which the present is passive – rather it can only be understood if we enter it and add to it. One of the great errors of our age is to think otherwise – to consider those as experts who hold a tradition up as something already past and able to be understood in a post-mortem fashion. The *life* and *living intellect* of the tradition is only to be experienced by those who are prepared to conjoin their own lives with it – those who, in the words of Socrates as he comments on the symbolic truth of myth in the *Republic,* have made "the greatest sacrifice." For to sacrifice is to make sacred, and to offer up one's own understanding upon the altar of wisdom is the required oblation for the Platonic philosopher. Such an attitude is regarded with suspicion by those who consider the weighing and measuring of objective facts as not only the summit of human reasoning, but also its sole proper employment: but the original understanding of the nature of philosophy by its earliest exponents led Porphyry to say, "Beatific contemplation does not consist of the accumulation of arguments or a storehouse of learned knowledge, but in us *theory must become nature and life itself.*" It is in this spirit that the following three dialogues must be accepted or rejected as the reader sees fit.

The Platonic tradition is both old and young but the vital subjects to which it addresses itself are those of perpetual importance to rational beings such as ourselves – the nature of the human self, of the good life, of the great universe in which we find ourselves, and of its source. In these three new dialogues we find these subjects discussed in earnest: the self as the soul, the happiness we seek, the divine ideas that underlie the manifested universe are all examined with a view to how the Platonic tradition might answer some of the positions adopted by modern thinkers. Answers are offered but in such a way as to stimulate the reader's own thoughts about these matters – and this is the key to the tradition: for unless questions are genuinely thought through by the reader, any answers suggested by the author are merely another set of opinions. But the true philosophic tradition is the safest of all paths to wisdom and happiness because it does not seek to impose a pre-digested body of concepts upon its followers.

If these dialogues are indeed an "endeavour after beautiful attainments", you as a reader are invited to make your own endeavour, and pursue wisdom as the birthright of a rational soul. Only in this way does the tradition maintain its integrity.

Tim Addey, 2011

Introduction

It should be clearly stated in the first place, that my motivation for writing these dialogues, however such motivation came about, was simply that of wishing to give something back, as an offering, to the tradition from which I have gained so many and real benefits over the long years. Likewise, as it now appears to me, my debt to Socrates, whether the unknown soul or as known to us through the corpus of Platonic dialogues, and to Plato is difficult to measure, yet is very considerable and unforgettable.

In assuming Socrates and Plato, these two remarkable men, and others, as the main speaking characters in these dialogues, nothing else is intended than a celebration of them and of the obvious inspiration they enjoyed, and of the subjects they will have from necessity considered. Academics, by far better qualified than I shall ever be, will continue to examine the works of Plato whether for facts, or truth, or justification for their own theories; and in this, I have merely attempted to imagine certain occasions that may or may not have happened, and certain subjects of conversation that may or may not have been examined and rigorously explored.

The situations involved in this little book are purely imaginary, yet it would seem very possible that a self-inflated, envious and wealthy sophist may have taken the opportunity to attempt to humiliate and subjugate Socrates when he appeared to have the weight of the world upon his shoulders, and when he was considering the import of the indictment unjustly raised against him. Likewise, it does indeed seem possible that Socrates may have engaged in some conversation with a servant who attended upon him during his final days, especially if this servant was such as held the behaviour and demeanour of Socrates as worthy of respect and most honourable and amicable. It also appears most probable that Socrates and Plato would have had a final time and conversation together, whenever that was and whatever were the subjects of their discussion; and that there must have been a more profound reason, other than physical sickness, that prevented Plato from being present at the last earthly moments of his beloved teacher.

But it must be said that, whatever the subjects discussed in these dialogues, or in those that have come down to us through history, it is the truth that is being sought and pursued, no matter who has written or announced it. For this is the obligation placed before all genuine lovers of wisdom by Socrates, Plato, their interpreters and all ardent philosophers throughout cultures and times – to pay little attention to who has said what about what, but to whether or not what is said or written contains anything of the truth, and, if so, what it is and why, and, if not, why not.

Through imitation, I am praising the heroes of a heroic tradition; and through assuming their names and characters, I am offering the most sincere thanks for all the real and lasting benefits received over so long by so many; and I apologise to them for the poverty of diction and thought when compared to theirs and to the profound beauty of their timeless works and days. Yet, in and for the love of wisdom, this little work is offered as a token of deep gratitude.

"Without the Gods how short a period stands
The proudest monument of mortal hands,"

The Iliad of Homer, Trans A Pope

THE THERAPON

A DIALOGUE

ON THE NATURE OF IDEAS

THE

THERAPON

PERSONS OF THE DIALOGUE

CRITO   PHAEDO

SOCRATES   THERAPON

SCENE: The precincts of the Temple of Hephaestus, overlooking the Agora, the morning after Socrates had died from poison.

CRI.   Greetings, Phaedo; though I dare to say that no matter the humour of this day, you, and I in truth, have but little to welcome, and even the sun itself appears diluted in power since the departure of our greatest companion.

PHAE.   Aye, friend Crito, this is easy to discover both from my mien and posture. I am emptied by the loss, and know not what best to say or to do in order to heal this angry wound within my heart.

CRI.   I understand, and if it were not for the sublimity of his temperance and courage, in the midst of such adversity, I too would believe that only prolonged mourning would be left in the place that he has vacated within us. But hear, friend, what my thoughts are now, after such a long night of exercise, and see if they can be of any assistance to us both.

PHAE.   I would gladly hear your thoughts, Crito, in preference to my own, if thoughts in reality mine are, and not merely the wild associations of a passive imagination, tormented by opposite opinions and phantasms, undisciplined and running free.

CRI.   I recognize those horses, Phaedo, and have wrestled with them all throughout this dreadful night.

PHAE.   I bear with me in my soul, like a branded image, a constant remembrance of the courage and temper exhibited by that man, both

4 *Release Thyself*

yesterday, and for so many days now past; and, perhaps, this impression will never leave me. But that virtue by which he surpassed all men known to me – that light which he so freely shone upon those who requested it, though he would say it was but dim – is what is now disappearing from my sight, like a ruined mirage at the approach of sunset.

CRI. To what do you allude, my friend?

PHAE. I allude, dear Crito, to wisdom, *his* wisdom; though he would again say that he possessed little or none.

CRI. If we can but remember his words, they will adumbrate with certainty the wisdom of that man, and, indeed, that soul which it imbued so beautifully.

PHAE. His words are not difficult to recall, but their true meaning surely is. For it appears to me at this moment, that words uttered by one or another in whose company one happens to be, and this regularly, carry more weight and are charged with so much more power than any that are recalled to the memory, or are written, or are reported by some other. In that dear man, soul and reason were always present together; so that what he was he said, and what he said he was.

CRI. Your judgment is spoken fairly; and he, on many occasions, declared either as a hypothesis or a conclusion, that soul itself is reason, and that of an undivided intellect and life.

PHAE. This too I recall, but with not a little irony.

CRI. Well said, Phaedo; but punish yourself gently and with prudence, as all of us, his friends and disciples, are enclosed in that same recollection.

PHAE. I will try to do as you suggest, but, for me, that last day passed more swiftly than any day should; and what is left in me, as an unwelcome residue, is a longing that I did not request of him that which most pressed upon me then, and for many years previous to that baneful day.

CRI. Speak, friend, and unburden yourself, for now it is surely our time.

PHAE. This I well know, and know even better how poorly fitted I am for such a time; and maybe only Plato, and one other, are truly prescient of what shall be required of us.

The Therapon 5

CRI. But he has gone from us for a period, as a wounded creature retires to allow a natural healing after a savage encounter; and this other, who should he be?

PHAE. One of but a very few; but enough of this, Crito, my regret presses hard upon me.

CRI. What regret do you mean, and what deep longing fills your heaving breast?

PHAE. That I, among all those close to him, did not request a simple and comprehensive demonstration of that which he discussed throughout our time with him, and that I could use, both for myself and for the benefit of others, if I could only both assent to and believe it.

CRI. You know as well as I that for him, things truly simple required a strenuous effort to express; and things comprehensive, a mutual energy that would not be diverted from its necessary end.

PHAE. That is sure, I know, but even now my regret persists with vehemence.

CRI. Be open, good friend, and tell me the nature of your regret, or lock it away safely and consider it in yourself. For the man is departed, and though we choose not to follow him into death, we ought to the utmost of our ability follow the dominating principle of his life; which even now, knowing the man, I am sure he is amply pursuing, once his period of rest and refreshment is complete. Phaedo, good man, explain to me what is in your mind, and why it troubles you so much.

PHAE. You are very good to me, Crito, and I appreciate your sympathetic indulgence, when you too, I know, are suffering from such a monumental loss as that which we witnessed so recently. I will try to be clear, and do you not exclaim with surprise that I should be so unsure about these things, after so long an exposure to their presence.

CRI. The indulgence is shared between us equally, and little would promote surprise in me after that of the day just past. Speak openly, friend, for you are safe in this company, and your uncertainty also may well be equally shared.

PHAE. That it may, Crito, but how will we see?

6 *Release Thyself*

CRI.   Declare, if you can, the nature of your uncertainty, and with whatever assistance he has left with us, we shall press for some comfort in the matter.

PHAE.   It is thus, my friend, and no more, for my doubts are concerning ideas, and they are grave. For as so many discourses that we shared with him, so many times did I desire to hear him declare what they truly are, and how they subsist, and what are their generations, and how they are contacted and participated. These my doubts are mountainous, Crito, and my shame in expressing them is proportionate.

CRI.   It is well and often said that shame ill suits a man in need, and especially when this indigence concerns a nature so profound, as well unknown save to some happy few. But I think that until the night before he took his final draught, I too was deeply involved in frequent doubt concerning these same things.

PHAE.   What is it you say? Are your doubts then all removed?

CRI.   For a large part they are, but not completely; and you will well remember the frequent assertion of his, that these things must be visited again and again and again, until they are more familiar to us than our own hands and feet.

PHAE.   I remember.

CRI.   Yet by some remarkable coincidence of need, or by a truly divine prompting, he took me with him on his final earthly visit to these things, and the journey and the way are still clear to my sight, so avidly did I listen, and follow and learn.

PHAE.   What does this mean, and how did this come about? For we were together that day before, and shared in the same discourses, even though so much time was given over to the comfort of his family.

CRI.   That is so, Phaedo, but we did not depart from the prison together.

PHAE.   Did we not? My memory is not to be trusted at this present time.

CRI.   We did not. For, late as it was, I went back to that place to ask that all conveniences should be extended to Socrates during that last night of his. And further, I prevailed upon the servant to let me sleep near to the precincts of his cell, as he is known to me, in order that I may be ready at the earliest moment to visit with Socrates, on what transpired to be his final day with us. Hence, I slipped into a troubled and shallow sleep, and awoke in some dark hour of the night, alerted by the closing of his cell door.

PHAE. For what purpose was the door closed at such an hour, and on such a night?

CRI. It was the servant, Phaedo, entering the cell, for the purpose of bringing to Socrates a drink. For, I heard him offer a generous thanks to the man, and an apology for having disturbed his vigil. But it was then that a most astonishing conversation ensued, between the servant and our greatest friend.

PHAE. This relation is truly remarkable, Crito; but tell me, please, what their converse involved.

CRI. I will, and it is by far the more remarkable as it concerned the very subject about which you, and innumerable others, suffer so many and frequent doubts and uncertainties. Their dialogue was concerning ideas.

PHAE. In the name of Zeus! Crito, this is more than coincidence or accident so called. Do you remember what was said, and clearly?

CRI. I do; and I recall it as if I was present to it now.

PHAE. I earnestly implore you to relate it all to me, as fully and completely as is possible, for I need to hear this more than anything else at this time.

CRI. You are not alone, Phaedo; for I need both to recall and to relate it, and thus generate from that seed a meadow true and vitally abundant.

PHAE. I feel the power of the sun increasing once more. Let us retire under the shade of this broad plane, and you shall generate, and we shall attend that meadow, the Gods willing.

CRI. They are willing. Come, sit here, and be at peace with yourself, and I will relate to you all that I heard.

PHAE. I am now in active peace, and will hold on to your every word. Speak on, Crito.

CRI. I will speak, and we will both listen; but the dialogue thus began:

* * *

8   *Release Thyself*

SOC.   I commend your attention to me at this hour, for you must be tired from the labours of your day.

THER.   Not so, master, for I do not think that I shall sleep this night, and to attend on you is not a burden. But I appear to have interrupted your work.

SOC.   Do not concern yourself, for the work that I planned is all but completed. What troubles you, man, that you cannot rest, though the moon is now high upon her course?

THER.   You have troubles enough, sir, without enquiring into mine, and which compared to yours are not important.

SOC.   That is difficult to judge; but my own are not unique, and are shared by all that are from mothers born. Come, sit with me, for time is short, and unconsciousness is not the rest I seek.

THER.   The advice to such as serve like me, who upon the departing waits, is to be brief and civil but to avoid any intimacy. For, as you say, the time is short, and not for the making of new bonds.

SOC.   Sit, man, my bonds are for me to choose to tie or to loosen, and by my word I shall not relate our time to your employers.

THER.   Thank you, sir, I will.

SOC.   What is it then that spoils your sleep? What keeps you so vigilant throughout each hour of the night? And, please, call me Socrates, for your company is a comfort.

THER.   Two things, Socrates, provoke this unrest in me. The first is common to many at this time, and concerns the sentence that has been passed upon you. In the taverns I frequent, all the talk is about your guilt or innocence of the stated crimes; and of why your accusers are so vehement in calling for your death. For, to most of the working folk, these charges seem ridiculous, when compared to what may have been said against you, and your education of those who brought many and deadly changes upon our ancient city.

SOC.   I understand what you and they say; but if I had in truth really educated those men, they would not have proceeded as they did. Their education was but in its infancy. Yet, as with infants given mighty power, they used it for their own ends, and put aside all that I proposed to them. If they had but held to what they began to discover, a quiet life is what they would have chosen. It was their ignorance that led them, and for this they are responsible, not me.

THER.   This is what the commoners agree upon, for you are more akin to us than to your accusers, we say.

SOC.   I am akin to any that admire and pursue truth, good man.

THER.   I have heard that it is so, and if this is the case, why then have your accusers forced you to accept the cup? Are they not friends of truth also?

SOC.   For their part, it is probable that they indeed hold this opinion; but if you could question truth herself upon this matter, who can tell what answer would be given?

THER.   But, Socrates, are not truth and justice allied, if any things are? And is it just that you are condemned now by a lie?

SOC.   By Zeus! Therapon, your questions are indeed profound, and would be well put to all those that have accused me. In short, I can only agree with you that truth and justice are allied; and if this, in reality, is the case, then it follows by necessity that untruth and injustice will also be allies, and appear to become a powerful allegiance, in breadth if not in depth.

THER.   This well points to the second provocation of my unrest.

SOC.   If the first is rescinded we should be grateful. What then is this second?

THER.   Forgive me, master, I forget the time and place, and I am ashamed that I bother you with these matters, when you are in such a difficult position. So much so that most men, in my experience of this process, can hardly think at all, far less engage in conversation. Is it your wish that I should be quiet, and leave you to your own inner converse?

SOC.   Beautifully said, my fine man; but this converse suits me well, and the time and place are most suitable for the consideration of these things that now trouble you. Please say on, and let us try to put to rest your second provocateur.

THER.   What I say now, I say for many who frequent the streets of Athens and labour with their backs and hands. When the mood, and aye, the grape takes us, we discuss these things among ourselves; and very often such discussions end in anger, or insult, or some other ribaldry. But

10 *Release Thyself*

I wish not for such ends, and would know how best I should examine these things. My meaning is this: we say, maybe with no great examination, that truth and justice are real, and are of the Gods; but what of untruth and injustice, evil, and such like things? Are they also real, and of the Gods, if we are to believe all that we hear about them?

SOC. Is this what troubles your rest, good man?

THER. It is, and other such like questions.

SOC. Would that these questions troubled our rulers and legislators, and kept them away from sleep's domain. What, then, would you have us do? Is it that we should examine together whether truth, and justice and other like things have an existence of their own – so as to be truth itself and justice itself? And whether that these same things are divine? And then to consider whether in a like manner there is error itself, and injustice, and evil itself, and the like, and that they too are from a divine allotment?

THER. If you consider me to be worthy and able, there is nothing I should desire more at this time.

SOC. Your worth is revealed by the nature of your question; and whether either of us will be able to discover the answers to your questions, will become most clear as we proceed.

THER. I hold a deep doubt that I will be able to follow you, unless you adapt your energy to a simple man like me.

SOC. It is not my energy that will determine our success, for we must both lift our heads on high, and not expect that great things should come down to us, like the stars descending to earth; for disaster lies that way. So come, man, let us make a beginning, and stretch our selves to this sublime work.

THER. I will endeavour to follow wherever you lead.

SOC. And I will endeavour to lead whence I am led, to the benefit of our simple souls. But are you happy to answer, as succinctly as you are able, to the questions that I pose as we proceed?

THER. I am very happy to do so, good sir.

SOC. Then we will make this beginning. Do you say that any thing a man can contact with the power of sense possesses some being, or existence, whether it can be seen, or heard, or touched, or tasted or smelled?

THER. I do.

SOC. And when you say that this same thing has being or existence, do you not say that it *is*?

THER. Again, I do, it is certain.

SOC. And is it the same thing to say that a thing is, and that the thing has being or existence?

THER. I firmly believe that it is the same to say these things.

SOC. And is this being, which is contactable by the senses, of such a kind as to be permanent or transient?

THER. I am not sure that I fully understand this present question, and for which I sincerely apologize.

SOC. There is no need for an apology, good Therapon. It may be well if we should choose some example, to act as a paradigm for this part of our investigation.

THER. I think that would indeed be well, Socrates.

SOC. Shall we then look to this flower, left by my friends, as a paradigm for this present time?

THER. In this bare cell, it is the only lively example I think that we could choose.

SOC. There may be a multitude of others we could choose, but let us see as we proceed upon this path. This flower, then, do you say that it is, and that it possesses some kind of being?

THER. I do.

SOC. And, to repeat, is this being of the flower of such a kind as to be permanent or transient?

THER. I consider it to be transient, and so much so, that it will hardly see out the coming week.

SOC. How then shall we describe this flower – as something that always is or as something that sometimes is?

THER. My lot is cast so that it sometimes is.

12 *Release Thyself*

SOC. If, then, it sometimes is, does it not follow that it sometimes is not?

THER. That clearly follows.

SOC. And to which of these states do we ascribe the monarch's share? That it sometimes is for a longer period than it sometimes is not; or that it sometimes is not for longer than it sometimes is; or that it sometimes is and sometimes is not for an equal measure of time?

THER. I have not considered this sort of thing before. But, as I reflect, it appears to me that it *is not* for a longer period than it *is*.

SOC. And is this period very extended, or is it such that it *is not* only for a limited period, and then it *is* again after only a little less time?

THER. I do not think it is the latter. I think the period is extended, and this extremely so. For now that I consider what you ask, it appears to me that this flower *is* only for a very short period, and that it *is not* for the remainder of time.

SOC. Do you say, then, that this flower *is* but once, for however long a time that may be, and that it never is again throughout the endless river of time?

THER. I now firmly believe that I do.

SOC. And do you also say that before this flower *is* it *was not*, and that after this flower *is* it *will not be*?

THER. I would not have known it before, but yes, I do.

SOC. But what do you then say, that while this flower is, *it is*?

THER. Yes, that is what I say.

SOC. What, then, do you answer to this?

THER. Ask, Socrates, and I will readily tell if I can.

SOC. Is it that you say that for so long as this flower *is*, you will never say that it *is not*?

THER. I will not.

SOC. But I see a conundrum on our horizon at this moment.

THER. How is that? What puzzle do you see?

SOC. I will tell you. If I heard you aright, you say that for so long as this flower *is* you will never say that it *is not*?

THER. I do so say.

SOC. What then? Is this flower, in all its detail, the same as it was yesterday, or the day before that?

THER. No; I believe that of necessity some changes will have occurred, even though they may be difficult to measure.

SOC. And what of its condition tomorrow, or the next week, or the following year? Will this flower be the same as it is now?

THER. It cannot be so, for the next year this flower will be no more, and by the morrow some changes will have occurred.

SOC. What, then, does this mean, and follows from what you have affirmed?

THER. I am not sure, but I suspect that it is nothing of a trifling nature.

SOC. I share your suspicion, good Therapon, and perceive it is something like this.

THER. Such as what?

SOC. If this flower is not the same as it was yesterday, nor the same as it will be tomorrow, or the next week, when do you then say that this is the same flower?

THER. I say that it is the same flower now.

SOC. And is it the same as it was at the start of our dialogue, and will it be the same as it is now when our dialogue has finished, for howsoever a short or long a time as that may be?

THER. It will have changed somewhat I allow, but I think that it must be the same flower.

SOC. And that in every detail?

THER. No, not in every detail.

SOC. Then would you say that this flower is *similar* to itself in its previous condition?

THER. I would and do.

14　*Release Thyself*

SOC.　But that it is not the *same* as itself in its previous or future condition.

THER.　It is not.

SOC.　What, then do we call that which is not the same with any thing?

THER.　If I follow your question aright, we call that thing different.

SOC.　What now do you say of this flower? Is it that the condition it is now in is *different* from that in which it was, and from that in which it will be in the future?

THER.　I do.

SOC.　But that at this *now* in time, you say that this flower is?

THER.　Again, I do.

SOC.　What, then, do you say is different from being, or from the condition of that which *is*?

THER.　I say that what *is not* is different from that which *is*.

SOC.　But, to recall, do you then still say that this flower *was* and *will be* different from what it *is* at this moment?

THER.　This I still say.

SOC.　But if it was different to what it is now, and will be different to what it is now, could it not be said that according to the past and the future, difference dominating, it will not have been and will not be, but that it only is as it is for the now?

THER.　I think that it could be so said.

SOC.　And do you define the now as something that is capable of being measured?

THER.　I do not see how it could be, for as soon as we attempt such a measurement it is past.

SOC.　I follow you. What then of this flower; do you say that it is and is the same only for an immeasurably small period of time?

THER.　I can only conclude that I do.

SOC.　And further, that it is not and is not the same for all of the time past and for all that is to come?

THER.   This is inescapable, though it does not donate a good feeling.

SOC.   That will follow, good man, if we can but find the truth. But let us see if we can obtain some anchor in this swelling sea. From what you have said so far, this flower both is and is not at this moment, as well in the past and in the future. But what prevents this?

THER.   Prevents what, Socrates?

SOC.   That it has become what it is, and is becoming to be what it will be.

THER.   Nothing that I can perceive prevents it.

SOC.   And would you say that even at this now, it is becoming to be what it will be?

THER.   I would say this, and I do.

SOC.   And will this hold good for every moment of this flower's existence, that it is always becoming to be, and will not remain the same as that which it was, and that which it will be? For its *was* was becoming to be what it is, and its *is* is becoming to be what it will be; and what it *will be* is becoming to be what it will not be.

THER.   Do you mean death? And that it *will be* becoming to be dead?

SOC.   What say you, Therapon?

THER.   I can find no other conclusion to our reasoning, but that this flower is always becoming to be, and that at its end it becomes what it is not.

SOC.   This is indeed a wonderful flower that we contemplate. I cannot believe that it was not left here for this very purpose. But come, good man, let us review our position. This wonderful flower then, whilst it lives, is in a state of becoming to be, but never is the same for even a fleeting moment, and both is and is not in a similar manner for however so long it exists; and yet is never the same with itself throughout this existence. Is this a fair summary of what we have discovered?

THER.   It is fair, though even now I feel I am on shifting ground.

SOC.   While we remain here we are both in that condition. Are you happy and able to continue?

THER.   I am. But here in my cloak I have some wine, reserved for this very night; will you share a little with me?

16   *Release Thyself*

SOC.   I will, and gladly, just so long as you promise that we shall not end this dialogue in an onslaught of tavern-like ribaldry.

THER.   Ha! You have my word we shall not, good master.

*

SOC.   What you reserved for this night has served us well. Are you then collected again, my friend?

THER.   Yes, indeed, and prepared now for the journey ahead.

SOC.   May, then, the Gods smile on our preparation and journey. Again we return to this flower, which is in a lifelong state of becoming to be. What more, then, can we say of it, and its existence?

THER.   Very much more could be said of it, but I would hear your thoughts as our leader.

SOC.   Then answer to this, if you will.

THER.   You need only to ask the question.

SOC.   Do you say that this is one flower, or otherwise?

THER.   I say that it is one flower.

SOC.   And when apprehending it do we perceive one thing or many things?

THER.   One thing is my immediate answer.

SOC.   And what will be your answer after a moment of reflection? Does it remain the same?

THER.   I believe that it does.

SOC.   Is it such a one as to be simply one alone, or does it admit of having parts?

THER.   It does indeed possess parts.

SOC.   And are these parts few in number, or are they many?

THER.   Now that I consider it, the parts appear to be many.

SOC.   Will, then, all these parts be apprehended by the power and sense of sight?

THER.   For the most part, yes.

The Therapon 17

SOC. What then remains?

THER. That its scent will not be known thus, nor will its taste.

SOC. How, then, will we know whether it is hard or soft, or cold or warm, or moist or dry, and other such like things?

THER. Without a doubt it will be from touching it.

SOC. And if it was to emit any sound, no matter how quiet or small, and which we at present cannot perceive, but yet understand that all motion produces some movement in its surroundings, would that not be apprehended by the power and sense of hearing?

THER. It certainly would, but it appears totally quiet to me.

SOC. It likewise appears so to me. But it may be that at some future time, the ingenuity of men might devise an instrument or tool adapted to this purpose, if necessity or desire requires it.

THER. You predict a subtle tool, Socrates.

SOC. I do. Would you say, then, that this flower is one whole consisting of many parts, and that these parts are perceptible to the senses?

THER. I would, and I do.

SOC. What then are its greatest parts?

THER. I am not sure that I understand this question.

SOC. I will try to illustrate it more clearly. See this, my sandal, what do you say that it is made from?

THER. Some bovine hide, or leather.

SOC. And is this to be considered as a great part of its composition?

THER. Nearly the greatest.

SOC. Yet, was this sandal to be found on the animal's hide as we perceive it to be at this moment?

THER. That would be profoundly useful, but it is absurd to say that it was.

SOC. Absurd, indeed; how, then, has it acquired its present appearance, if not generated by the hide itself?

THER. It can only be through the art of the sandal-maker.

18 *Release Thyself*

SOC.   And would you say that this sandal-maker possessed an image in his mind of the sandal he desired to create? Or would he work on the leather without thought or plan, and trust to chance that a usable sandal would be produced?

THER.   There is not an art in trusting to chance; and I clearly know from my cobbler friend that he works from the image in his mind.

SOC.   And if that image is of a fine and useful sandal, will he not strive to make one as near in perfection to that image as his art and skill permit?

THER.   He will.

SOC.   So would you say that together with the appropriate hide, the image held by the artificer is also a great part of its composition?

THER.   That is certain, and is at least as great as the hide itself.

SOC.   Do you say, then, that the material of this sandal, and the image of it in the maker's mind, are two of the greatest parts in its composition?

THER.   I do, if not the greatest.

SOC.   And what if this sandal perishes over time, is it possible that its maker would be able to produce another one, nearly the same or similar?

THER.   Very much so, as this is his art and his living.

SOC.   How could that be?

THER.   He will repeat the process as nearly as his art allows him.

SOC.   And this by looking to the same or similar image, and by working the same or similar material?

THER.   Very much so.

SOC.   And can this repetition be achieved a few or many times?

THER.   As many times as he desires, and for so long as he retains his art.

SOC.   This image, then, beheld by the maker, is capable of frequent reproduction of similars.

THER.   It is.

The Therapon 19

SOC.   And this for so long as the image is retained, the material is available, and so far as the art is able to be practised?

THER.   Yes.

SOC.   And what if this sandal should perish, will the image perish likewise?

THER.   Not for so long as the sandal-maker lives, and preserves his sanity.

SOC.   That is well said, Therapon. Could we, then, call this image in the sandal-maker's mind the form of the sandal to be made?

THER.   We could, and happily.

SOC.   What now do you say are the greatest parts of this sandal?

THER.   From our reasoning, I can only say that the leather and the form are nearly its greatest parts.

SOC.   And would you further say that the sandal is a whole composed of parts?

THER.   I would, with certainty.

SOC.   And what of the form?

THER.   What of it?

SOC.   Is this not a whole also, and is it not previous to the production of the sandal?

THER.   I am sure that it is, and is held before the production commences.

SOC.   And will it yet remain after the sandal or sandals which are made in its image are made, and have then perished?

THER.   It will, for so long, as I said a few moments ago.

SOC.   It is well. But my foot becomes cold sooner than the appointed time. Shall we then return to the flower?

THER.   By all means, Socrates.

SOC.   Recall, then, that you said this flower was a whole composed of many parts.

THER.   I recall.

20 *Release Thyself*

SOC. Do you recall also that I asked, what, then, are its greatest parts?

THER. I do.

SOC. Does an answer now present itself to you?

THER. If I consider what we just now said regarding your sandal, and apply it to this flower, I should think that whatever it is made from is one of the greatest parts.

SOC. And what do you say that it is made from?

THER. I hardly know what word to use, or how it is best to define it.

SOC. But would you say that it is made from something or from nothing?

THER. From something, it must be so.

SOC. It must. And is this something capable of being composed into the appearance of this flower?

THER. Again, it must be, or it would not be here, or becoming to be here, at all.

SOC. You learn well, O good man. But see if you can answer me this. When this flower begins to perish, do we not say that it decomposes?

THER. We do.

SOC. And does it not then begin to lose its scent, and shape, its taste and texture, and its ability to move or grow?

THER. Without any doubt it does.

SOC. And further, when it is finally perished to the point that it can do so no more, do we not say that it has decomposed?

THER. We do, and rightly so.

SOC. And that the flower is no more?

THER. It is no more.

SOC. What then is left behind of it, when the flower is said to be no more?

THER. Whatever it was made from.

SOC. Can you ascribe a name, now, to this whatever?

THER. I cannot; but it is the stuff that all such things are made from.

SOC. Could this stuff be called the material that all such things are made from?

THER. It must be.

SOC. And in its simple uncomposed state, is it any more the material of a flower than of a tree, or of a horse or a goblet, or any thing else of this kind?

THER. I have never considered this before; and at the moment I am unsure how to answer this question.

SOC. We will proceed gently, and with caution. The meaning of my question is this; when the flower is finally decomposed and reduced to the simple material it was made from, and likewise the horse and the tree, and the goblet and other such things of that nature, would you say that the material of each of these was the same material, or that each is composed from a different material and one specific for every individual thing?

THER. I cannot agree to the latter. Hence, I own that the material is the same or very similar for each and all of these things.

SOC. Then do you say that it is not flower material, or horse material, or goblet material, or material belonging to any thing else but to itself?

THER. I do.

SOC. Then it is material itself, or can you name it otherwise?

THER. I cannot, and I am happy with that name.

SOC. And do you still hold that this material is capable of being composed into the body of a flower, or a tree, or a horse or a goblet, or a myriad of other such things?

THER. I do so, very much.

SOC. It is here, then, that we must cross the threshold with vigilance, as is whispered in our ceremonies.

THER. I am vigilant, Socrates, like never before.

SOC. We shall proceed in that spirit. Will this material, then, possess the power to compose itself?

THER. Compose itself into what?

22   *Release Thyself*

SOC.   Into a flower, in the first place.

THER.   How can it? For it knows not what a flower is.

SOC.   Or a tree, in the second place?

THER.   My answer is the same, and will be so for all other similar things.

SOC.   Again, do you say that this material possesses the power to compose itself?

THER.   It has not.

SOC.   Then it would seem to possess one power alone.

THER.   What do you say that is?

SOC.   The power of being itself and nothing else.

THER.   I agree wholeheartedly.

SOC.   But in being itself, is it not capable of being composed into the appearance of other things?

THER.   Very much so.

SOC.   But it does not itself compose itself into the appearance of other things.

THER.   It does not possess that power, I am sure.

SOC.   This, then, will be its nature. But we are come to a mighty question now, my friend, and it is this. What then is it that composes this material into the appearance of being other things?

THER.   If you please, Socrates, before we proceed, I believe that I need some more wine, to calm the rush I feel coursing through me. Will you join me?

SOC.   I will, you deserve it, my friend; and I thank you.

*

THER.   Time is passing, are you happy to continue now?

SOC.   I am, for there is ample time to come to some answer to your questions.

THER.   That is good, very good.

SOC. If then we are calmed again, will you answer me the question – what is it that composes this material into the appearance of so many other things?

THER. Even with this wholesome wine, and good as it is, I am unable to offer any answer.

SOC. It may be that you will be able to answer me this, Therapon.

THER. What is the question?

SOC. If this material does not possess the power to compose itself, does it not follow that there must be some power or powers which do compose this material?

THER. There must be such a power, I think, or none of these things would exist as we see them.

SOC. And this power, if it is not the power of the material, must it not follow that it is the power of something else?

THER. It must follow.

SOC. And this a non-material power?

THER. Yes.

SOC. Is that which is not material called immaterial?

THER. It is.

SOC. Then do you conceive that the power which composes this material is an immaterial power?

THER. I do.

SOC. But this immaterial power appears to have at least one other allied to it.

THER. And what do you say that it is?

SOC. We have said that there is something immaterial which has the power to compose material, have we not?

THER. Yes, we have said this.

SOC. What then, would you say that this power which composes material must know what that is into which the material is to be composed?

24 *Release Thyself*

THER. I would.

SOC. And yet another power is now appearing above our horizon.

THER. What power is that?

SOC. The power of being itself a power.

THER. Again, I see that this must be so.

SOC. Then do we not have these three immaterial powers, that is, the power to be, the power to know, and the power to do?

THER. Yes, and wonderfully so.

SOC. Wonderful indeed, my friend; and further, these powers, being themselves immaterial, can they be perceived by those faculties which we, in our present condition, use to apprehend material things, that is, our senses?

THER. How can they?

SOC. Then being immaterial, are they not invisible, inaudible, intangible and the rest?

THER. They must be so.

SOC. And being immaterial, they are not composed from material?

THER. They are not.

SOC. And not being composed from material, are they then subject to material decomposition over time?

THER. Again, they are not.

SOC. Shall we now summarise, and take stock of our present position?

THER. Please do, Socrates, for it is a good one I believe.

SOC. We seem to have agreed then, that all things composed from this elemental material that is perceptible to the senses, are in a lifelong condition of becoming to be; and that this same material is incapable of composing itself into any thing else, or into the appearance of any thing else; and, also, that an immaterial power or powers composes this material into the appearance of all these things which we perceive in the material universe, and that this same power cannot be contacted or apprehended by our senses. Is this a fair summary of our landmarks so far?

THER. It is very fair.

SOC. Then let us proceed, for I think we are at the midpoint of our journey.

THER. And a pleasing journey I consider it to be.

SOC. That is good. Consider this, in the next place, if you will my friend.

THER. Consider what?

SOC. The nature of this immaterial power that composes material things; can we yet name it?

THER. For my part, at this moment, I cannot.

SOC. But there are very many, and some lauded by the wealthy and famous, who say that they can and do name it; and nothing hinders that there will be many more in the future time who will embrace this popular opinion.

THER. What name, then, do they give to this power?

SOC. *Chance*, they so denominate this power, and it pleases them to name it so.

THER. Many times I have heard it so called, by the sober and the intoxicated alike.

SOC. Perhaps there is but a small difference in their condition. But we should try to see what they can mean by this; as the popular view, though it may be unexamined, deserves no little attention at times, and especially when it is promoted by the learned.

THER. I agree, very much, that it does.

SOC. We may not, then, be able to give an accurate definition of so tricky a power as this chance, but it will not be beyond our wit to discover some of its principal characteristics, do you not think?

THER. I think that we should be able to, Socrates.

SOC. This lauded chance, then, do we not say that it is peculiarly unpredictable?

THER. We do.

SOC. Do we not likewise say that it appears to be uncertain?

26 *Release Thyself*

THER. Again, we do so say.

SOC. Does it not also appear to be random?

THER. It does, very much so.

SOC. And what of accident; do we not also ascribe this to chance?

THER. This, also, we do.

SOC. Briefly, then, among other things, we consider chance as being unpredictable, uncertain, random and accidental; is this a fair description of it from common rumour?

THER. I think it is very fair.

SOC. And will it not follow that wherever chance dominates the more in any thing, these very characteristics will likewise be the more dominant?

THER. How could it be otherwise?

SOC. And likewise, do you think that where chance dominates the less in any thing, that these characteristics will also be less dominant?

THER. Again, I believe that they will.

SOC. Then what of chance itself?

THER. What do you mean?

SOC. My meaning is, what of this chance that totally dominates, will not these characteristics be likewise totally dominant?

THER. They must be.

SOC. And would we not say that what something is or does to others, in the first place, that it is or does this to itself, and this totally?

THER. Again, it must be so.

SOC. The essence of this chance then, if such it truly is, must be to itself totally unpredictable, uncertain, random and accidental. Or do you think that it can be otherwise?

THER. I do not think that it can.

SOC. And must it not then be to all other things totally unpredictable, uncertain, random and accidental, though these same things should evolve forever?

THER. I am sure that it must be so.

SOC. We appear, then, to have a universe of this nature.

THER. Of what nature, Socrates?

SOC. Of a material that is incapable of composing itself into the appearance of any thing else, and the composing power of chance that dominates this same material.

THER. I know not what to say of this vision.

SOC. That surprises me but little, yet, we will take one step further.

THER. And I will endeavour to attend you.

SOC. If, then, this composing power is chance, possessing totally the characteristics we have attributed to it, will not the things that it then composes from this material exhibit these very same characteristics?

THER. It cannot be otherwise.

SOC. And further still, if chance is the principal and only composing power of the universe, will not all things be dominated by its characteristics, and this as far as even to time itself?

THER. Without exception, this must surely follow.

SOC. Then do we find ourselves in a universe where everything is unpredictable, uncertain, random and accidental, and where no one thing can be relied upon for anything or for even a single moment.

THER. It is a dire universe you describe, Socrates.

SOC. And can we not say this, of the man who holds this position to be true?

THER. Say what?

SOC. That this principle of chance will likewise be dominant in him, so that every thing he is, or does, or thinks, or feels, or believes, or loves, or aspires to, or is attracted to, will be unpredictable, uncertain, random and accidental; and that according to these he will lead that type of life, and will expect to find the similar in all those that he associates with, and that they and the universe will deal with him in a similar manner.

THER. In truth, this is now a very dire man you have described.

SOC. And can we find this man anywhere?

28 *Release Thyself*

THER. I think we cannot, though there are those who say strenuously that they hold to this belief.

SOC. They do so say, but they do not so live.

THER. Thank the heavens that they do not.

SOC. But, Therapon, must not the converse of what we have asserted also be considered?

THER. And what is that?

SOC. We have predicted, my friend, the condition of things where the more of chance will be dominant; but what then will be the condition where the less of chance is dominant?

THER. I say that the being unpredictable, uncertain, random and accidental, and other similar things, will likewise be the less dominant.

SOC. And what will be the condition of things if chance is removed entirely? Will it not be that of being predictable, certain, ordered and definite, and everything else of this kind?

THER. It will be thus, most certainly.

SOC. And are there those who hold this position to be true?

THER. I have heard that there are those who say as much.

SOC. And do they so live their lives?

THER. They do so, if then they are divine.

SOC. You speak beautifully now, dear Therapon.

THER. Yet I am all but speechless.

SOC. Are you then fit for the final part of our journey, until another time?

THER. I am feeling full of energy and enthusiasm at this moment.

SOC. That is very good. But we should look once more at that condition which we called *becoming to be*.

THER. And I am glad that we must do so.

SOC. Would you now say that it follows, that whatever is in the condition of becoming to be is also in a condition of change?

THER. Yes, I would.

SOC. And could we say that this change is not such as from one thing into another different thing, but such as from a similar to a similar?

THER. We could, and we do.

SOC. And is it from what it was, to what it is?

THER. It is so.

SOC. And is it then from what it is, to what it will be?

THER. Again, I am sure that it is.

SOC. What, then, do you suspect is the condition of something before it even was?

THER. Socrates, I am not at all sure how to reply to this.

SOC. Take this slowly, my friend, and consider again what I ask. Before this thing was, what can we say of it?

THER. I can only suspect that it was not.

SOC. Following on from this, what then will be the condition of this thing after it will be?

THER. I can only conceive that it will not be, or that it has been.

SOC. These, then, appear to be the generations of that which is becoming to be, or is subject to this type of change: from that which was not to that which was, from that which was to that which is, from that which is to that which will be, and from that which will be to that which will not be. Is this what we have now discovered?

THER. We have.

SOC. And do you say that the condition of that which *was* is similar to the condition of that which *will be*?

THER. I do.

SOC. And what of the condition of that which *was not*: is that also in a similar condition to that which *was*?

THER. It cannot be so, for to me they appear to be opposites.

SOC. And what of the other? Is the condition of that which will be similar to that which will not be, or is not?

THER. This again appears to me to be the condition of opposites.

30   *Release Thyself*

SOC. And do we not say that, in general, opposites are different?

THER. We do.

SOC. And that there is but little of the similar to be found in them?

THER. Again, we do so say.

SOC.   Thus, indeed, is this process of change truly difficult to apprehend. For it appears to be this: to be from that which was not into that which was, to that which is becoming to be leading to that which will be, and into that which will not be. The surrounding enclosure of the similar is thus removed from the process of becoming to be, or change. For the cause of this process is different from it, and is non-existent; and the end of this process is also different, and is equally non-existent.

THER.   I know not where to turn now, Socrates, nor what there is left to hold on to.

SOC. Then we should attempt to restore the enclosure, good man.

THER. In truth, we should.

SOC.   Is there, then, anything of the similar in that which always was and that which was?

THER. They are indeed similar.

SOC. And is this the case also, with that which will be and that which will always be?

THER. It is the case, I am sure.

SOC.   And can we find the similar in that which is, and that which is becoming to be?

THER. We can, and I do.

SOC. The process of change now appears to be thus: from that which always was to that which was, from that which is to that which is becoming to be, and from that which will always be to that which will be.

THER. It does so appear.

SOC. But must we not admit of that which always was, that it cannot of itself become that which sometimes was?

THER. Very much we must.

SOC. And of that which is, can it become that which is becoming to be?

THER. It cannot.

SOC. What then of that which will always be: can it become that which will only be sometimes?

THER. Again, I do not see how it can.

SOC. Which of these, then, depends upon the other for its existence?

THER. I feel I am short of breath, Socrates, so please enquire for both of us.

SOC. I will do so, as the time is now advanced. Is it then possible for that which only sometimes was, to have any existence without the presence of that which always was? And can that which is sometimes becoming to be have any existence without some connection to that which always is? And can that which will be sometimes, subsist without that which will be always?

THER. I can breathe and see clearly now, and it is like the sun is coming up; and my answer is that they cannot.

SOC. We will allow it. Do we then say that the condition of the sometimes was, of the sometimes becoming to be, and of the sometimes will be, can be attributed to the same one thing, such as this flower?

THER. We do.

SOC. And that this could be said of many, if not all, of things of a similar nature?

THER. It could and should be so said.

SOC. And could we then say that the condition, if such it is, of the always was, the always is, and the always will be, can be attributed to some same one thing?

THER. We could so say, but of what I am not yet certain.

SOC. Could it not be said of something eternal, that it always was, always is, and that it always will be?

THER. Ha! It most certainly could.

SOC. Then consider in yourself whether this should be said of many, or of all, things of a similar nature.

32 *Release Thyself*

THER. I am in no doubt at all that it should.

SOC. Does it not then follow, that whatever sometimes is must be totally dependent upon whatever always is for its existence?

THER. It does, and happily so.

SOC. And will it also follow, that whatever always is must be totally dependent upon that which simply is, in order to be at all?

THER. This is very thin air, Socrates, and I am in need of your hand.

SOC. You have it, and we shall fly together. Can we then say that what sometimes is denotes a temporary being?

THER. We can.

SOC. And can we say further, that what always is denotes an eternal being?

THER. This also we can.

SOC. Then does it not follow, that whatever simply is, without any addition or condition, must denote that which is primarily being, and is being itself, and is alone?

THER. Heavens above, Socrates, this place is now become astonishing.

SOC. I cannot but agree. But it is time to draw in the net, if we can, and see what we may have caught.

THER. Whatever assistance I can give you is at your service, master.

SOC. Then let us apply ourselves to the task with superhuman energy, if we can. But before we do, we should consider two more things.

THER. And what are they?

SOC. Whether we should be able to attribute a similar generation to that which lives, and to that which knows.

THER. I believe that we should try to.

SOC. Does it then follow from our previous reasoning, that whatever sometimes lives is generated from whatever always lives; and that whatever always lives receives this power from that which simply lives, and is life itself?

THER. It follows, and wonderfully so.

SOC. And here is another wonderful thing, that according to this investigation, that which sometimes knows will be generated from that which always knows; and that whatever always knows receives this power from that which simply knows, and is knowing itself.

THER. Truly, I see that this must very much be so.

SOC. Of necessity, I too believe that it must be, if our reasoning is sound. If we can but accustom our sight to these things, we should attempt to look to them directly and ask: are these then three of those immaterial powers that we have just recently discovered, that is, the power to be, the power to live, and the power to know?

THER. They very much appear to be, and are great powers I would add.

SOC. And would you say that powers are the powers of something, or the powers of nothing?

THER. Surely they must be the powers of something.

SOC. What then will be that something of which the *to be* is seen as the power?

THER. If I apprehend this correctly, it is the power of that which we just now mentioned, of that which simply *is*, or *being itself*.

SOC. And what is that something of which the *to live* is said to be the power?

THER. It can only that which we said was *life itself*.

SOC. And will it be similar in the case of that something of which the *to know* can be seen as the power?

THER. It will be so, and that something is *knowing itself*.

SOC. What, then, do we say of this?

THER. Of what, Socrates?

SOC. Do we say that being itself *is*?

THER. Yes, and very much so.

SOC. And that life itself also *is*?

THER. Certainly.

SOC. And that knowing itself likewise *is*?

34 *Release Thyself*

THER.   Likewise.

SOC.   Then we appear to have caught here three beings, exhibiting three powers, all of which are immaterial, and generating the always, the sometimes, and the becoming to be.

THER.   We have, I fully agree.

SOC.   So does it now follow that whatever possesses the appearance or the reality of being sometimes, or is becoming to be, living sometimes, or knowing sometimes, that these powers are derived from those things that *are always, that live always, and that know always?*

THER.   It follows, without any doubt.

SOC.   And are these then, to be always, to live always, and to know always, generated from that which simply is, that which is simply life, and that which simply knows?

THER.   I now believe that they are.

SOC.   And what of these can we say further? Is this being itself one being?

THER.   It is.

SOC.   And this life itself, is it one life?

THER.   Again, it is.

SOC.   And this knowing itself, is it one knower?

THER.   Very much so.

SOC.   And further, would you say that if the *one* were removed from all of these, that they would then disappear, as they would no longer be even one thing?

THER.   I would.

SOC.   It is well that we are silent then, for just one moment, as we are near to that upon which all these things depend, and of which we can say little more.

THER.   This small silence is extremely full.

SOC.   Now, Therapon, when we look again at this sandal of mine, which is of the nature of some composed material; what was it we said was the other great part of its appearance?

The Therapon 35

THER. The image or the form of it in the sandal maker's mind.

SOC. You remember well; and would you say that, according to the form of sandal that the artificer possesses, he can produce many sandals and of many types and designs and colours and materials, and the like?

THER. I would so say, and that for as long as he lives, and possesses the ability to make.

SOC. Then you should now transfer your attention to this flower, and see how it appears to us now.

THER. It begins to look profound, Socrates.

SOC. Your perception reflects yourself, good man. But did we not say that the material from which it is composed does not possess the power of composition?

THER. Yes, we did.

SOC. And this in a similar manner to the hide from which the sandal was made, that it did not have the power to make the sandal?

THER. In a similar manner.

SOC. Was it necessary then, that there should be a sandal maker, in order that the sandal could be made?

THER. It was.

SOC. And that without the presence of this man or woman, the sandal maker, the sandal itself would never be produced by the hide alone, though the hide should exist for an infinite time?

THER. It never would.

SOC. And will this be the case with every object that is man made and material, such as a cloak, or goblet, or a staff, or a crown and all things of a similar nature?

THER. It certainly will.

SOC. And is it that although these materials should always exist, no one of these things will ever be produced without the presence and art of the man or woman who can make them?

THER. It is so. They will never come about without these types of people.

36 *Release Thyself*

SOC. Again, then, we return to the flower, and ask, is this flower man made?

THER. In no manner can we say that it is.

SOC. But still, does it appear to us to be a flower, for however so long as it exists?

THER. It does.

SOC. And what of the material from which it is composed, and which does not possess the power of composition, though it may exist throughout all of time – is it not powerless to produce this flower?

THER. It is.

SOC. And are there similar flowers to this one, and flowers of other kinds with other names, and these so many and so various?

THER. There are very many.

SOC. What then? Do we say that there is the material from which all these flowers are composed, but that there is not any one composing form of them?

THER. We may try to, but, in truth, how can we?

SOC. Your answer is a resounding question, Therapon. But what of this form? If it is not to be found in the material itself, is it not then immaterial?

THER. It must be.

SOC. And if it is immaterial, and, therefore, not in a condition of becoming to be, to which of these states do you ascribe this form?

THER. Which states do you propose?

SOC. The ones that we apprehended earlier – I mean, that which always is and that which never is; to which of these do you ally this form?

THER. I cannot see in any manner how that which sometimes is, or is becoming to be, can be the offspring of that which never is and is nothing.

SOC. That, indeed, is difficult.

THER. Then I am certain, at this moment, that the form must be of the kind that always is.

The Therapon 37

SOC   What name, then, would you give to this form?

THER.   I would denominate it flower, or the form of flower.

SOC.   And is there a limit to the number of flowers, or species of flowers, that may be generated according to the form or idea of flower?

THER.   How can there be?

SOC.   Yet the limit of them all is simply that they are all flowers, no matter how many may rise into existence.

THER.   It is so, though their number should be beyond counting.

SOC.   And would you say that whatever qualities any flower may possess or express, that these are received from that same idea or form of flower?

THER.   I would, and very much so.

SOC.   And further, that these same various qualities, when they are impressed upon the material, do they then become perceptible to the various powers and organs of sense?

THER.   I think that they do.

SOC.   If, then, we say that any thing is deformed, do we also say that this is received from the form?

THER.   How can it be? For that which appears to be deformed must be without that form, or deprived of it to some degree or other.

SOC.   Either that, or something else must be present to that which appears to be deformed.

THER.   What can that be?

SOC.   That which many say they believe to exist: the form of deformity or deformity itself.

THER.   That has an evil sound to it, Socrates.

SOC.   It does so, Therapon, but we should not fear to examine it. If, then, deformity itself exists, would not its very essence and being be deformed?

THER.   It would.

SOC.   And what of its power or powers, would they not likewise be thoroughly deformed?

38 *Release Thyself*

THER. They would, and very much so.

SOC. And its energies, whether they are in doing or knowing or anything else, would they not also be deformed to the same degree?

THER. Again, they would be.

SOC. And can we say that what is deformed is complete, and is a whole, and yet is deformed throughout itself?

THER. I am not sure how to answer this.

SOC. Is, then, a deformed whole the same as a whole?

THER. It is not.

SOC. Then would you say that it is different?

THER. I would.

SOC. What then is it that is different from a whole, or do we not say that it is a part?

THER. We do.

SOC. Then the deformed is a part — is this what follows?

THER. It appears that it does.

SOC. But as a part, must it not in this also be deformed?

THER. It must.

SOC. And a part is not the same as a deformed part?

THER. It is not.

SOC. It is then different to a part.

THER. It is.

SOC. What then can we call that which is not a part of anything, and yet is not the whole of anything either?

THER. I cannot find a name for something of this kind.

SOC. That is not surprising, for it appears that wherever this deformity itself is present, it is deformed even in that presence; and that at its very essence it is deformed, and this totally; so that we cannot say that it *truly is* to any degree, except as the result of the absence or distance from, or the distortion of, form.

The Therapon 39

THER. I now understand what you are saying.

SOC. If, then, deformity itself is the absence of form, it can never be a form; and if it is the distance from form, it will be an appearance only, and sometimes is and sometimes is not, and occurs in the material but not in the form. For how can that which is without form be the same as that which is form?

THER. It cannot be.

SOC. And how can that which only appears as the absence or distance from anything, or is the result of the distortion of something, have anything but a passing or fleeting presence, and which is at once removed when form is totally present to the material?

THER. It cannot but have that temporary and partial appearance.

SOC. Then we are now approaching to the purpose of our investigation, and I will propose to you this further question.

THER. Please propose it, Socrates.

SOC. Do you say, then, that anything is true, or that nothing is true, or that some things are true and that some are not?

THER. I would say that some things are true, and that some are not.

SOC. And would you say of these same things, that those of them that are true *are* true, and that those of them that are not true *are not* true?

THER. I would.

SOC. Do you say, then, that what is not true exists?

THER. I am not sure what answer to give, Socrates.

SOC. Then consider this: do we not say of that which is not true, that it is not?

THER. We do.

SOC. And do we not say of that which is sometimes true, and sometimes not, that while it is true it is, and while it is not true it is not?

THER. Again, we do so say.

SOC. And what of that which is never true, can it be said that it ever *is* at all?

THER. It cannot be said with any sanity.

SOC. But what of that which is always true, will it not always truly be?

THER. It cannot be otherwise.

SOC. Do you see, then, that such as is the truth of anything, such is its being?

THER. I do, and very clearly.

SOC. And that where there is no truth of any thing, there likewise there will not be being?

THER. This too I clearly see at this moment.

SOC. Then are we left with that which for a time is true, and that which is always true; and that which for a time is, and that which always is. Do you also see this?

THER. I do.

SOC. What, then, do you say that ignorance is?

THER. It is the state of not knowing something.

SOC. And of this not knowing something: do we not say that it is the not knowing of the truth of something?

THER. We do.

SOC. And do we not say also that if we know something, we know the truth of that thing?

THER. Again, we do.

SOC. And that the truth of something is what that thing is; do we say that this is so?

THER. We do.

SOC. Then is the truth of something altered or affected by whether we know it to be true, or are ignorant of its truth?

THER. How can it be?

SOC. It will still be, and will still be true, then, whether all men know it or all men are ignorant of it?

THER. It will.

SOC.   But is it possible that some one of men will believe that something is true when it is not, and that he or another will believe that something is not true when it is?

THER. This happens many times, and with very many men and women.

SOC.   If, then, either of these men act according to these beliefs, will they not act in error, and according to their ignorance?

THER. They will.

SOC.   And acting in error, will they then act justly?

THER. I cannot see how they can.

SOC.   And in acting unjustly, will their actions be good or otherwise?

THER. They will be otherwise.

SOC.   Can we now say, then, that where there is the lack of truth, there also will be the lack of justice and goodness?

THER. We can.

SOC.   But that where truth flourishes, justice and goodness will flourish likewise?

THER. I do agree.

SOC.   So what of that which we say is good; if it is indeed good, is it not true that it is good?

THER. Most certainly.

SOC.   And will it be the same with that which we say is just; that if it is indeed just, is it not also true that it is just?

THER. It is.

SOC.   So that truth is truly true, and goodness is truly good, and that justice is truly just; does this now appear to be the case?

THER. Again, it certainly does.

SOC.   Look, then, with me for a last time upon this flower. Do you say that it is true in its becoming to be?

THER. I do.

42 *Release Thyself*

SOC.   And would you say that it is just to itself, and others it communicates with, in that all its parts contribute some good to the whole?

THER.   Though I have not considered this before, I would indeed.

SOC.   And in its appearance and properties, would you say that it has some goodness, and beauty and vitality?

THER.   Very much so.

SOC.   So that its truth, justice, goodness and the like, while present with it make it to be what it is, and prevent it from becoming deformed and decomposing; would you agree to this?

THER.   I would and do agree to it.

SOC.   They then possess a guardian power, as well as one that is productive?

THER.   They do.

SOC.   Then we must come to a conclusion, for I have a little work left to do before the rising of the sun.

THER.   That will be good, Socrates.

SOC.   We have discovered, then, that where the form of truth is so there will be existence. And further, that where truth is always present, existence or being likewise will always be present; and that in so much as anything is true, so it will be just and good. We have also found that there are immaterial forms and ideas, which are eternal in themselves, and possess the power to generate, compose, guard and provide for all things that are of a material or temporal nature. And, finally, that the deformed, the untrue, the evil, the unjust and other things of the like kind, do not possess a being of their own, but are only generated for so long and in so far as anything is distanced, for whatever reason, from form, truth, goodness, justice, and all other things that are eternal, and always live and know – for these are truly living beings, ideas themselves, and are permanent, immutable, beyond change and beyond chance, and they will remain so whether all men are ignorant of them or not. So that in as much as all of these are, and each of them truly is, *one*, this very one will appear to be the God of each and every eternal being, and makes all these things to be divine, and without which being itself is not possible, and to which we owe nothing but gratitude. Now, then, if ever, let our silence be the symbol of what cannot be spoken.

* * *

CRI. And at this moment I heard a movement, and a sigh profoundly deep, followed by the sobbing of that good servant, Therapon.

PHAE. I am so moved and truly delighted to have heard this sublime relation of yours, dear Crito; and it has helped to heal the wound within my heart. But tell me, was this the very end of their converse?

CRI. Very nearly.

PHAE. What else, then, did they say?

CRI. It is not easy to repeat it without tears, as I very much experienced at the time.

PHAE. Please, Crito, make the attempt for me.

CRI. Then I will, Phaedo, and their converse ended thus:

* * *

THER. Socrates, truly the dearest of men, I know not what to say, or how to thank you for what you have done for me this night. But I cannot, in all justice, perform the duty for which I was appointed to you, and which the judges demand to be done.

SOC. It is just that you should, good Therapon, and none other would I have to prepare and to pass me the cup. Now that I know you, I am most certain that you will do your duty well, and will neither delay nor misjudge it when the appointed time arrives. You will not do me harm, and I would prefer in an eminent degree to be served thus by a friend, and not by an enemy. So be of good heart, my friend, and remember all that we have said, for in this is my salvation, as it is for all our kind; and I rejoice in the good time to come.

*

CRI. With these words Socrates turned to the table, and proceeded to complete the work he had intended to do; and the servant departed in tears, without speaking anything further.

44 *Release Thyself*

PHAE. This conversation has re-empowered the sun, and I would, with you, examine all its meaning and import. Have you time, and to spare, this day?

CRI. I have.

PHAE. Then let us together seek out Plato, and any other of our friends, and share your inspired report with them. But, what is this? I see that very Therapon approaching, cloaked in the garb of one who wanders.

CRI. Good Therapon, where are you now going?

THER. I am going in another direction from that of my time so far.

PHAE. What do you mean by this?

THER. I am gone from the prison for good, and will never return to that place. I wish now, and for all my time to come, only to attempt to be that which Socrates was and is in truth.

PHAE. And what do you say that is?

THER. A philosopher, and a friend of truth.

PHAE. So come with us, good man, for there is one that you should meet who will assist you on your way, and is in truth that wisdom's lover.

THER. Then I will follow you, and meet with him, and never leave his side.

*

* * *

THE ALPHAEUS

A DIALOGUE

CONCERNING HUMAN HAPPINESS

THE

ALPHAEUS

PERSONS OF THE DIALOGUE:

ALPHAEUS   TELAMON

SOCRATES   A WOMAN

SCENE: The precincts of the Temple of Zeus, below the Acropolis. Socrates has just been informed of his indictment for corrupting the youth of Athens, and is sitting beneath an olive tree, deep in meditation.

ALP.   I see now before us the very image of a philosopher; poor, unkempt and much in need of wisdom I suspect from his demeanour.

TEL.   Yes, I see him too, the mighty Socrates; as ever Atlas-like, bearing the weight of the world's errors upon his ample shoulders.

ALP.   I think that his own are now added to that weight, and may well prove to be more than even he can support, though no doubt he would die in the attempt.

TEL.   Do you wish to speak with him, Alphaeus, or shall we pass him by on the left, and leave him to his solitary task?

ALP.   Very few things in this life are free, except for the conversation of Socrates, who, had he the means, would even pay us to be the subjects of his hectoring, so much does he desire to enlighten poor souls such as ourselves.

TEL.   Poor indeed, Alpaheus; but poverty sits ahead of us seated under an olive, and we should not be backward in donating to him some sort of wealth, as between us we possess more goods than he can imagine, both of the body and of the mind. Let us be generous, and share our store with him.

ALP.   I agree, good Telamon. Hail, Socrates! I would ask if you are well, but your condition now surrounds you like a millstone.

48   *Release Thyself*

SOC.   Greetings, Alphaeus, and I am indeed well, thank you.

ALP.   You know Telamon here, I am sure, who is my patron and a man of great generosity.

SOC.   I do, though it is many years since I have seen him. Greetings, Telamon, and I trust that Alphaeus is proving worthy of your patronage.

TEL.   Very much so, Socrates, as I am sure you would have too, if you had only accepted my offer those many years ago.

SOC.   That is a kind thought, Telamon, but I cannot agree with it; as even now my opinions are not popular, and maybe even less so than they were then.

ALP.   But the opinions of one who has so obviously benefitted from his pursuit of wisdom, are more popular than you now conceive, and are the cause of much hilarity to those who discuss and debate them.

SOC.   It appears that you can see inside my soul, good Alphaeus; and it gratifies me to know how well my views are received by those that have heard them from others. If they are the cause of such happiness I am content.

ALP.   When they can be remembered they surely are, Socrates. But what ails you on this fine morning, for you appear to be surrounded by a cloud?

SOC.   That is ever the case with the ignorant, Alphaeus.

TEL.   You have said as much so many times, but your pretence to ignorance is worn like a symbol of honour.

SOC.   I was not speaking of myself, noble Telamon.

TEL.   Of whom, then, were you speaking?

SOC.   Of those who perceive clouds where there are none, and those who imagine sunlight where there are only impenetrable clouds.

ALP.   And do you include us in that incisive observation?

SOC.   How can I know?

ALP.   How, indeed, Socrates, unless you wish to discourse with us and discover the truth?

SOC.   That is ever my wish, Alphaeus; but discourse, to me, is not a competition.

ALP.   I share that sentiment, as to me it is a great source of happiness.

The Alphaeus 49

SOC.   Then you are indeed fortunate it seems, in having discovered such a wonderful source, and one that is so readily available.

ALP.   And it is a source not only of happiness, but of comfort and companionship, wealth and pleasure, and all other good things that a man needs. Is this not the case with you also?

SOC.   You are even more fortunate than I understood at first, if not only you have discovered such a source of happiness, but that you have also conceived what it is that a man needs.

ALP.   You know my meaning, Socrates, so do not be trite with us. I state only what is obvious to all, in saying what a man needs in order to be happy.

SOC.   And is this what you sell to your admirers, and to the audiences that surround you?

ALP.   It is but a small part of what I have to offer.

SOC.   Then the remainder must be indeed magnificent; but tell me, please, is it your opinion, then, that a man can be truly happy in this life?

ALP.   It is.

SOC.   And others too, and all men?

ALP.   All, without a doubt.

SOC.   Are you then happy, Alphaeus, and you, my noble Telamon?

ALP.   I am, and completely so.

TEL.   And I am so likewise, especially since my association with Alphaeus, from whose instruction I have gained so many insights and pleasures.

ALP.   But what of you, Socrates? Answer the same question that you just now asked of us; do you then say that you are happy?

SOC.   Now that I consider it, I am not sure what answer to give, or even if I agree with your assertion that any or all men can be truly happy in this life.

ALP.   Why do you doubt it, as the proof is talking to you now?

SOC.   I do not doubt that you believe yourself to be a happy man.

ALP.   Ever you speak in the same manner, Socrates, as one who knows the condition of another better than that other himself.

50 *Release Thyself*

SOC.   How can that be, Alphaeus? For I openly admit that I do not know your condition, or that of Telamon here; but only that I accept that you both believe that you are truly happy.

ALP.   Cease your dissembling! It is only fit for children and the immature. I do not *believe*, I know!

SOC.   We are in sacred precincts here, and I much more fear the wrath of Zeus for what I say than that which you are now displaying. Stay happy, Alphaeus, and sit down here, and talk with me; or depart in peace and leave me to my meditation.

ALP.   Forgive my indignation. I meant no dishonour to you or to this holy place. But what would we talk about, Socrates, that you cannot meditate alone?

SOC.   That which you just now mentioned in passing, as if it were nothing but common knowledge, and upon which I meditate frequently.

ALP.   And what was it that I mentioned?

SOC.   It concerned happiness; and appeared to me to be the statement of one who knows in what the nature of true happiness consists, and how it is to be attained by all men in this life. Is this what you have just now asserted?

ALP.   It is.

SOC.   And are you willing to share your insights with me, and our friend Telamon, who still stands beside us in silence?

ALP.   I am most willing; though Telamon here has heard me discourse upon these things many times.

TEL.   Yet not so many as I would not be pleased to hear them again, especially on this day and in this place.

ALP.   Sit then, Telamon, with us, as we have some time before my first appointment.

TEL.   I will, and gladly.

SOC.   Are you ready, then, to instruct me in these matters, upon which I confess I am even now uncertain?

ALP.   I am ready, Socrates, to assist you out of your uncertainty. What would you have me say?

SOC.   Only the truth as you perceive it.

The Alphaeus 51

ALP. I will do so with no little enthusiasm, if you will but ask me clearly what you now wish to know.

SOC. Thank you, Alphaeus; and in the first place it is this – what is it that you say happiness truly is?

ALP. A simple question deserves a simple answer, and it is this, Socrates. Happiness is the state of the man who has satisfied his desires, and whose desires are thus fulfilled.

SOC. My question was indeed so simple as to be barely apprehended, as I asked not of human happiness, but only what happiness truly is. But perhaps it may be that nothing else can be or become happy but man.

ALP. I assumed you did not wish to spend my precious time and energy investigating the happiness of snails and dogs, or camels or the like.

SOC. Or even trees and flowers, and the very planets and stars themselves; but it is of no matter, for it is happiness that we seek, and maybe you were correct in starting from ourselves upon this search. You say, then, that happiness is the state of a man who has satisfied his desires, and whose desires are fulfilled. Have I recalled this accurately?

ALP. To the syllable and to the word.

SOC. And do you maintain still that it is possible for a man to be truly happy in this life, according to your own or another definition?

ALP. I do so and very much, according to my definition, as I am not aware of any that is better or more universally acknowledged.

SOC. Maybe we shall discover some other as we proceed. But in the meanwhile, will you answer me this?

ALP. I will answer anything that you ask.

SOC. It was ever so, Alphaeus. But do you say that a man is then happy when all his desires are fulfilled, or that he is partially happy when only some of his desires are satisfied?

ALP. I say both, Socrates, and see your ambush well in advance.

SOC. That is acute vision indeed; yet I ask further, is it possible that all the desires of any man can be fulfilled?

ALP. It is, for they are small in number.

SOC. But not in power, perhaps; so will you name these few, for the benefit of Telamon and me?

52 *Release Thyself*

ALP.   I will, and they are these: wealth, power, a good family, good health, and a fine reputation.

SOC.   And you say that a man who has a sufficient portion of these will then be truly happy?

ALP. I do.

SOC.   But, again, I ask you, is it then the case that when anyone acquires only a part of these things, then that same person will be only partially happy?

ALP. You speak the truth, Socrates.

SOC.   Hardly, Alphaeus, I only ask for an answer.

ALP.   Then my answer is yes, that this will be the case with such a man.

SOC.   What, then, do you say of yourself? Do you possess a part of these things, or the whole of them?

ALP.   I possess enough of them to have satisfied my desires.

SOC.   Then it appears from what you are saying that sufficiency in these things will be the measure of a man's happiness, or would you say that it is otherwise?

ALP.   I say that the sufficient will be enough to satisfy a man or a woman's desires.

SOC.   And these very desires, Alphaeus, for wealth, power, comfort and fame, and all the rest, be they ever so gentle or vehement, do you say that they are satiable or insatiable?

ALP.   I own that they are satiable, Socrates; so that when a man has that which he desires he desires no more, and he is at peace with himself, and with all of those around him.

SOC.   Would you say, then, that this self-satisfied condition of peace is what you have denominated happiness?

ALP.   I would and do say this, as would every sane man and woman.

SOC.   And you, Telamon, being a sane man, do you concur with this definition of happiness?

TEL.   I do, Socrates, from my own experience, and from my observations of many people in many cities.

SOC. But further, Alphaeus, so that I may be very sure concerning what you affirm; do you mean to say that when a man has what he desires, according to your definition of what is desirable, then his desires are satisfied, he will be at peace both with himself and others, he will be truly happy, and that in this condition he will desire no more? Is this an accurate summation of your position?

ALP.   Socrates, old man, you pick at bones where there is no meat. Knowing your present and future dilemma, it little surprises me that you must repeat and repeat in order to try to find fault in my position; and your envy is obvious together with your dissatisfaction. *Your* desire for footless wisdom has got you to where you are now, and to the discomfort which you continually experience. But, yes, that is my position, and it is a very pleasant one; and had you but adopted it in your youth or middle age you would not be suffering as you are now, and contemplating some ignoble end.

SOC.   I accept these remarks, concerning my present and future condition, in the spirit in which they are offered, and I will bestow upon them the consideration and time that they deserve. But come, Alphaeus, let us not get distracted like a certain mule of Triphion, for we should concentrate on what we have begun. These desires, then, that you have enumerated, do you not only offer to your followers to name them, and to announce that they may be satiated, but do you also pronounce to them how these desires may be satisfied and in what manner they may be laid to rest?

ALP.   I do; for the way to the acquisition of wealth, health, power, good families and reputations may be taught, and taught well. For what I have done and achieved may be copied by others in the same or a similar manner, according to the vocation of each man or woman. If you doubt it, Socrates, I am sure that Telamon here would need little persuasion to fund your attendance at my courses, where you will see for yourself how simple it is to become happy, as I am now.

SOC.   I doubt that I have the aptitude or the time now to pursue these things in an appropriate manner; but I thank you for the offer on another's behalf.

TEL.   He only speaks the truth, Socrates, and you know that my affection for you is even now both open and generous.

SOC.   I do know that, good Telamon, and it is reciprocal. But come, let us proceed. Have you now, Alphaeus, numbered the primary desires upon the satisfaction of which true happiness is acquired?

ALP. I have.

SOC. And there are no others?

ALP. None that I consider to be so essential, and that are not the offspring of those I have announced.

SOC. But I see at least two more that, far from being some minor offspring, may well be the parents of the rest.

ALP. And what are they, Socrates, please tell?

SOC. The first is the very desire itself of happiness, or the desire to be happy.

ALP. Ha! You are like a child examining his supper, and exclaiming some eureka that his food satisfies his need, and that the desire for it is his motivation for eating. These common desires for nutriment or happiness are to be taken as granted, and can no more be removed from a man than his head or his heart. Leave them aside, Socrates, as you are only discovering the obvious, even at this late stage.

SOC. But even the obvious needs examination sometimes, Alphaeus, as it often conceals great and unapparent truth.

ALP. What do you mean by this laborious aside?

SOC. I mean that there is nothing more obvious than the sun, yet what man knows but the smallest part about its way?

ALP. We are not discussing knowledge, Socrates, but desire. So please be pertinent, if you wish to arrive at your destination.

SOC. Then I will, Alphaeus, and we will leave behind the obvious, and assume, maybe, that the desire for happiness is something of our nature, being unconscious for the most part, independent of knowledge, and not inquiring any further. For, perhaps, happiness when present is no great motivator, or when absent is merely the object of a basic need.

ALP. You wear perhaps and maybe like a veil, Socrates, to conceal your naked uncertainty. But what of the second desire you say that I have omitted; what do you say that it is?

SOC. I say that it is the desire to protect and preserve the acquisitions obtained by those other desires.

ALP. Again you pretend to discover something profound, and fail to see that the attendant desire to protect and preserve those acquisitions, is but

The Alphaeus 55

the offspring of the acquisitions themselves, and that their preservation is merely an element of their acquisition.

SOC.   Perhaps I do fail in this; but are to attain and to maintain two names for the same thing? Or is the attainment of something, and the maintenance of that thing, two differing operations?

ALP.   I grant that they appear to be different, though involved with the same desire.

SOC.   And you, Telamon, is this also your position, that the desire to attain or acquire something, is but semantically different from the desire to maintain or retain that same thing?

TEL.   I must confess that, at this moment, I am not as convinced as Alphaeus that they are but two sides of the same coin; but I would ask you, Socrates, to make more clear your thoughts.

ALP.   Be cautious, Telamon, you are inviting a wolf to cross the threshold of your house.

SOC.   By the huntress! You need not fear, good Telamon, and you, Alphaeus, for I am not a lycanthropist or anything of the like; but I own that to a timid and motherless lamb, there is little that does not appear to be threatening. But come, Alphaeus, answer plainly if you will: is the desire to attain and acquire something, the same as the desire to protect and preserve that thing? Or are they only the same because they are both of them desires, and that their difference is dominated by their different subjects?

ALP.   I will not rise to your taunts, Socrates; but I will answer you directly, and I say that the desire to attain or to acquire something is the paramount motivation here, but that the desire to maintain or protect that same thing is but the natural offspring of the former, and is obvious to all, save one or two unhappy envious souls.

SOC. I think I follow you, as I hope is the case with Telamon also; but we can be sure of what you say if we enquire further.

ALP. Press your case, Socrates.

SOC. Thank you, I will. For it appears to me and to anyone who knows you but a little, that you have in your life acquired some ample wealth, at least sufficient to satisfy your desire for it. Is this a fair statement, Alphaeus?

ALP. It is as fair as it is true.

56 *Release Thyself*

SOC. And would you say that this attainment of sufficient wealth has resulted in your condition of being happy?

ALP. I would say this, as it is also as fair as it is true.

SOC. But do you think that if you were to increase this wealth that your happiness would increase likewise?

ALP. I have already stated that I have sufficient, and that I have satisfied my desire for wealth, and that I am happy with what I have acquired; so that I do not desire more, and care not whether it may add any small increment to my happiness – for I am content, Socrates.

SOC. It maybe that you are, Alphaeus, and in that case I commend you; but consider this.

ALP. What is it that you bid me to consider now?

SOC. To what degree your happiness is dependent upon the preservation and maintenance of your wealth.

ALP. That is an unworthy consideration, Socrates; and you would be wise, Telamon, to dismiss it along with me. For I am happy, both in myself and with what I have acquired, and this no sane person can deny.

SOC. Strenuously asserted, my friend; but if I frame the consideration within a question, perhaps it will appear more palatable. Do you consider that your happiness, in this respect, is dependent upon the preservation and maintenance of your wealth?

ALP. Your question is no more palatable than it was in its previous disguise.

SOC. But it is a maskless question, and only requires some appropriate reply.

ALP. Then I reply that my happiness will be but little or not at all affected by some limited lessening of my wealth.

SOC. And if the lessening of your wealth is considerable, and very much so, would this have any effect at all upon whether you are happy or otherwise?

ALP. As this will never happen I can make no intelligent reply. For what is not possible is hardly worth contemplating.

SOC. Yet even with the great, this type of occurrence has proved possible, so imagine, if you can, this very considerable reduction of your wealth, and what effect upon your happiness may be produced.

ALP. You are impertinent, Socrates, and dominated by envy, thinking only the poor, such as yourself, can be happy; though this happiness is without choice or effort, and is clung on to like a crack in a cliff-face.

SOC. Is the mere thought of such a reduction in your means sufficient to produce some effect?

ALP. It is not the thought that is affecting me, it is you, and your dog-like gnawing at old bones.

SOC. Forgive me, Alphaeus, for the hungry love to gnaw. But, if you will, let us leave behind the subject of wealth, and consider some other of those few desires of man, and which you say that you have satisfied. What then of your health, and your happiness regarding its condition? In a similar manner, would you say that a considerable reduction in your good health would have any effect upon your happiness? Or do you say that this also is not possible, and, therefore, not worthy of consideration?

ALP. With the wealth that I possess, I shall be able to mitigate any bad effects of ill-health, in as much as it is possible; and the rest I shall bear as contingencies of life. Hence my happiness will be but little disturbed, save as it is for any man facing his expiry from this life.

SOC. But what, then, do you say now to this? How would the happiness of any man be affected if he is reduced to poverty, his health has failed, his power has no influence, his family disowns him for failing in his duties, and his good reputation has been turned upside down, and he is known only as poor, sick, powerless and alone? Do you still say that you would be happy, when all these desires, having been fulfilled, are then become unsatisfied and raw?

ALP. Fie on you, Socrates! What man could remain happy if all these things were removed, or whose desires were never satisfied in the first place?

SOC. What man, indeed, Alphaeus? But I have spoken of extremes, and it may be that the middle ground is safest. Suppose we find the man that has sufficient wealth for his needs, together with sufficient good-health, and power, and good family, and a good reputation though it be not broad or well known; is this the man, then, who is truly happy? And though he should lead a quiet life, and disturb none, and be a friend to many, will he thus be truly happy? Or will his happiness also be at risk, from the decrease or increase in his satisfaction of those universal desires you have nominated?

58 *Release Thyself*

ALP. This man would be happy in his own manner, and to the degree that his desires have been fulfilled; and this is the same as I said at the first, before you began your minute dissection.

SOC. But were he to verge to one extreme or the other, would his happiness be altered accordingly?

ALP. That it may be, for these desires unsatisfied lead to unhappiness, and satisfied to the desired degree will produce happiness.

SOC. Then do you now say, that the desire to satisfy these desires to a desired degree is the pathway that leads to true happiness?

ALP. I do.

SOC. But what, if each of these desires is unfulfilled, is it then possible for a man to be happy?

ALP. This would truly be a sad man, Socrates, who cannot satisfy his desires at all; and in him that natural desire to be happy would be all but impotent.

SOC. That may well be, Alphaeus, but at this point we cannot be certain.

ALP. But we can, Socrates, we can! For where will you find the man who does not desire wealth, and power, and health and family and reputation? Can we find him anywhere, or is it only you?

SOC. As I am still unsure of what true happiness consists, and how it may be attained, whether I have these desires or not, or to what degree they are useful or otherwise to this attainment is but of little value. Yet come, Alphaeus, and see if we can summarize what you say and teach. Is it that the desires of men are few in number, and are capable of being satiated and satisfied for so long as they are being fulfilled; and that the more they are fulfilled the happier that man will be, and that the less these same desires are fulfilled the happiness will be proportionately less? Is this what you propose to us all?

ALP. It is.

SOC. And that true happiness is only true for so long and in so much as these desires are fulfilled and satiated?

ALP. Again, I do say so.

SOC. But is not something that is true always true? Or will it only be true sometimes and for some periods?

ALP. You tell me, sagacious Socrates.

SOC. I will, as it appears to me, and that if something is sometimes true it is also sometimes not true; but if something is simply true it will always be that which it is.

ALP. And so what now? Where is this leading?

SOC. It is leading to the distinction between apparent and true happiness; and that the former appears and does not appear, but the latter simply is what it is. And further, that it is the path to the former which you sell and teach, but not the path to the latter.

ALP. It is ever your way to bring those down who possess more of anything than you, I well know this; and I not only teach the way to happiness, but also how it may be attained, maintained and retained, and it is true and happiness and true happiness – nothing more or less, and that is an end to it!

SOC. It is well, Alphaeus, that you are sure of what you do. But, if you would indulge me, please answer me one or two more questions.

ALP. I will do so if the time allows. What say you, Telamon? Shall we stay a while longer?

TEL. I do not know quite what to say at this moment, for this conversation is now resounding in my mind. But yes, Alphaeus, it would be good to stay for a little more time.

ALP. Then we will, Telamon, for your sake if not for mine. What is it then, Socrates, that you now wish to ask?

SOC. Only this, in the first place; would you say that there is a limit to what any man may desire?

ALP. Yes, there is; and it is the limit that a man imposes according to his ambition.

SOC. But that in itself, the desire will not naturally limit itself, but will desire to add to or supplant that which it has already successfully obtained?

ALP. That is probably so, Socrates,

SOC. And is it probable that the more a desire desires, and the more it obtains what it desires, that it will thus become stronger and more powerful?

ALP. That, too, is probable.

60   *Release Thyself*

SOC.   What then, is it that the more powerful and stronger the desire becomes, the more difficult will it be for anyone to impose a limit upon it?

ALP.   That is so.

SOC.   And do you teach each of your followers what is the appropriate limit for their desires?

ALP.   I do not, for that would be presumptuous and meddling.

SOC.   Then do they set their own boundaries according to their ambitions, and in so far as their desires are still capable of being limited?

ALP.   They do.

SOC.   But you do not teach how desires may be limited, whether gentle, or vehement, or greatly powerful?

ALP.   I do not, and I know not of anyone who does.

SOC.   That may well be so, Alphaeus; but you are in danger of releasing a certain Ate's dragon for yourself, for your followers and for us all.

ALP.   I know exactly what I am doing, Socrates, and you would do well to remember that in the coming weeks. But what is this creature of which you now speak, and have brought in from some obscure place?

SOC.   It is a tale from an island very much west of here, and one that I heard early in my youth; but to tell it may take more time than you will allow.

TEL.   Time is not yet pressing, Socrates, so please relate this tale if it has any bearing on this invigorating discussion.

SOC.   And you, Alphaeus, is this your wish also?

ALP.   If Telamon wishes to hear this story, I will wait patiently along with him.

SOC.   Very well; but as the tale is long I shall pare it down for brevity's sake, and for the sake of your patience, Alphaeus. A wise and beautiful good woman once told me all of this, and thus she began the story:

There are four islands near to the edge of our ocean where the children of the sea were born. Here, also, the ambiguous Eris gave birth to a lovely daughter, and she named her Ate. Some report that the father of Ate was Zeus, some that it was Poseidon, and yet others say that she was fathered by Pan. Suffice to say, that this immortal child was admired by all

The Alphaeus 61

who saw her, because of her exceeding beauty and grace, her all-affecting charm and happy demeanour. Yet, even from an early age, wherever she went disagreement and discord appeared to follow in her trail, and arguing and dissension fell upon those who were previously friendly to each other, disrupting their amicable union. No reason could be assigned for this, as the child said and did nothing contentious, nor ever seemed to be the cause of anything but pleasant and warm emotions when present; but still in her wake unwelcome division followed, and neither she, nor any who mixed with her, ever considered that she may be the cause of it.

In her early youth she gained the favour of wave-calming Zeus, who, even though he would not recognize any relationship to the immortal girl, was prone, because of her charming demeanour, to listen to her supplications. These, as you will know, lead to a lifelong trial for one great hero, and to her banishment from the divine courts, to be cast down back to the island of her birth and there to live out time, forgetful of the whole of her celestial family. Yet she was ever a happy girl, and as she matured into her fine young womanhood, she delighted equally in her solitude as she did in her contacts with her native islanders.

On one cloudless and azure-skied morning, she was walking along her favourite strand absorbed by the heat of the day, when she saw, not far out to sea, five dolphins swimming and playing. Removing her light attire, she walked through the warm gentle waves, and was soon among the dolphins, who reveled in her company, so well could she swim and dive and play. After an hour had passed in this sport, Ate looked toward the shore, and saw there a small cave entrance that she had never noticed before. Ever curious, she swam to the shore and walked up to the cave, having to get on her hands and knees in order to enter it. Inside the cave its walls and arched ceiling were as smooth as polished marble, and many tiny multi-coloured flowers grew in invisible cracks throughout its depth. After walking ten paces she came to a shining wall, and up above her there seemed to be a narrow shelf bedecked by even more brilliantly coloured flowers. Standing high on her toes, and slowly stretching to her fullest, Ate felt on top of the shelf, and her fingers closed on a large round object, which she lifted down to see what it might be. It was an egg; though not one like she had ever seen before, as it was perfectly round, perfectly smooth, and perfectly green. Removing from the cave, holding the egg out before her, she walked back to retrieve her clothing, and made her way to her solitary home beside the sparkling River Kygnos.

Every day and every night Ate observed the egg, but no changes could be perceived in its perfect form. A whole month passed, and, as the bright full moon coursed her way throughout the night, Ate was woken by a single 'crack'. Rising from her resting place she knelt down by the fireside, and saw to her astonishment that the egg had split in two, as if it had been cut by a surgeon's knife around its full diameter. But what astonished her even more was the sight of a small but intricately formed dragon, warming its opening wings by the embers of the fire. And not only was this dragon so utterly charming in its appearance, but it sang, in some unknown language, the most enchanting song imaginable; and it moved the young woman to tears of pleasure and of joy.

When at last the sun was up, Ate took the little dragon down to the nearby shore, and placed it on the warm sand within a ring of stones she used often for lighting fires and cooking simple food. As the dragon walked around the ring it happened upon a small pile of twigs that Ate had saved for kindling, and, after looking at it for a few moments, it blew a jet of fire out of its tiny nostrils, and the pile was consumed and reduced to ashes within just a few seconds. This delighted Ate, and she clapped her hands and laughed out aloud. The dragon, too, seemed very pleased with its display; but a moment later it began to utter a plaintive moan as it stared up at her, a pleading look in its jewel-like eyes, its breathing laboured as if it was worn and exhausted. Taking from her basket a small piece of bread, Ate offered it to the forlorn dragon, and it immediately snatched it from her outstretched hand, swallowed it whole, and then began to flap its wings and jump around in a circular dance. This also delighted Ate, and she laughed again at such a pleasant experience. Within moments the little dragon found a small unused branch, and, as before, after contemplating it for a short time, it blew out another plume of flame and consumed it to ashes in seconds.

One whole year passed by, and the dragon was now fully grown, and immensely powerful, and its appetite for consumption was beyond control. Ate was terrified of it, having long passed the point where she was delighted or amused or enchanted by its habits. Most of the trees, the plants, the crops and fruits, and animals and people of that island had fallen prey to the dragon's voraciousness, and those few islanders that were left either fled their homes in the dark by boat, and went for refuge to one of the other three neighbouring islands, or they hid in caves and hollows by day, and grovelled about in their search for food at night. Ate could no longer provide for its needs, and the dragon, though it did not try to consume her, ignored her, and would frighten her away by the mere look from its hungry eyes. Hence, she sought refuge in the little cave where she had found the dragon's egg, and regretted constantly that she had ever made that fatal discovery. And in the evening hours she would swim with the dolphins, and share with them their diet from the sea.

Unknown to Ate, all these events had been observed by three old and haggard women, who, by stealth and subtlety, had followed her every move, and had worked tirelessly to mitigate the evils which Ate had unleashed. But these aged ladies were there from a divine allotment, and reported to Zeus all that had transpired, and all that they had done for those who were threatened by such a general destruction. And he, in divine response, empowered these sisters to sow the seeds of revival below and above the ground.

One of these seeds was to make their presence known to the despairing, yet still beautiful, Ate. On a moonlit evening, when the ocean was calm and the stars appeared at their very brightest in their celestial round, Ate emerged from the sea, and made her sad way to the dragon's cave, there to dry and clothe herself, and cry from the torment of her guilt. Looking through her tears, she saw the three ancient sisters sitting in the entrance to the cave, silhouetted by the rising full moon. Ate did not know what to say, except, "Who are you? And why are you here?"

"We are messengers." One of the sisters replied.

"Which one of you said that, please?" Ate questioned in return, as the three females were surrounded by night, save for their silver outline.

"I did." Said another one.

"Why are you here?" Ate asked again.

"Because we are messengers." A third voice replied.

"Do you bring a message for me, or do you take a message from me?"

"We do." Was the reply of all of them.

"What message do you have for me?"

"The message that we are messengers."

"Who sent you here, good ladies?"

"One whom you have forgotten."

64 *Release Thyself*

"Who have I forgotten?"

"The one who sent us here."

"But what is his name, or her name, please?"

"It is the name you have forgotten of the one you have forgotten."

"I remember everyone, apart from who my father is, of whom I was never certain to begin with."

"Do you have a message?"

"How do I know what to say to one whom I do not know?"

"Do you have a message?"

"Then I do; please, please help me to destroy the dragon that is consuming all this land. Plead with him for me, I beg you ladies, please."

Without saying anything further, the aged sisters arose and departed as noiselessly as the mist upon the presence of the morning sun. For her part, Ate decided that she would try her best to talk to the dragon, and persuade it to cease its avaricious and mindless rampage.

For many weeks the dragon would only ignore her and fly from her every word, but eventually it sat down with her and listened to Ate's arguments, which were skillful and long and too many to repeat here. But for each of her arguments it had a better one, and though she tried her very best with all the reason she could muster, Ate could not convince the dragon on one or any point regarding its destructive behaviour, as it justified everything it did in a manner she could not overcome. Driven to despair, she returned to her little cave, while the dragon destroyed the last living things on the island, and then began to destroy the island itself.

One fine dawn, Ate awoke from a deep sleep, and saw at the entrance to the cave the three aged sisters silhouetted by the rising sun.

"Have you a message for me, please?" she asked.

"I have."

"Who is it from?"

"It is from one who heard your message."

"Is it from my father?"

"It is not."

The Alphaeus   65

"Who, then, is it from?"

"From one who knows your dilemma."

"What does he say?"

"She says to take this, and to use it well."

As the lady finished, she tossed a small disc-like object towards Ate, which glittered as it span through the rays of the risen sun. Catching the disc she examined it, discovering it was a two-sided mirror in the figure of a perfect circle. She was about to ask the purpose of the mirror, but saw that the three venerable ladies had already departed, their message delivered and their reason fulfilled.

Five more days passed, and the dragon had reduced the island to a small parcel, hardly bigger than itself and the cave where Ate had made her home. She waited until the dragon was asleep, and, shedding the ruins of her last clothes, she emerged from the cave and walked into the sea for her morning refreshment, the round mirror held carefully in her right hand. Never had she seen the ocean so calm, and flat and void of any movement save for the radiating ripples of her gentle swimming. Above her, the massive azure vault of sky was cloudless, the sun the only body in its vast expanse; around her, the massive glass-like sea, the minute island the only visible object in its answering expanse. Rising slowly from the water, deep in concerned thought, Ate once again examined the mirror, and silently prayed that she might discover its purpose and its power.

But she did not notice the dragon as it woke, and silently raised its gigantic frame to dwarf the beautiful maiden. It was, as ever, hungry to consume, and stared at Ate with a vile and unfeeling look in its eyes. She stood there alone, naked, and prepared for the onslaught to come, her tiny patch of island offering nowhere to turn; like the cry of Ajax to his faltering men, she heard his words resound again and again:

"This spot is all you have, to lose or keep;

There stand the Trojans, and here rolls the deep.

'Tis hostile ground you tread, your native lands

Far, far from hence; your fate is in your hands."

And without knowing why, Ate held up the mirror between herself and the great dragon's head. The first thing it saw was its own reflection, which just for a moment terrified it, as it had never before seen its own aspect, and especially this one, overcome with monstrous greed and the longing to consume. But as Ate shifted the mirror a sharp dazzling bright shaft of reflected sunlight burnt into one, and then the other of the dragon's massy eyes. It turned to shield itself from the brilliant beams, but too late, the damage was done, and the dragon was blind in both its eyes. Once its fury had abated, it turned its blind head to Ate and pleaded with her to look after it, and help and care for it, and to direct it so that it would not die. Ate agreed, and as the days passed, the dragon shrank back to the size it was when it first emerged from its green egg; and it listened to Ate, and obeyed her, and served her every need.

TEL.   And what then happened to them, Socrates?

SOC.   Zeus forgave them both, or so the story tells, and elevated them to the stars that move between Earth and the Olympic heights; and even now they can ever be seen on a clear night in the west, the beautiful Ate with the dragon at her feet.

ALP.   Well told, Socrates, and the meaning of your myth is clear. But I release no dragon with what I do, and even though I do not teach how desires may be limited, I know full well that they limit themselves according to the ambition of each individual.

TEL.   You are not being generous, Alphaeus; and I thank you, Socrates, for that tale, which appears to conceal much in its fine imagery; and even now it seems to me that ambition itself is a desire of no little power.

SOC.   The tale says much, Telamon, but it would take some long time to discover all its truth. But come, Alphaeus, let us continue our discussion, as you found my slight digression so unappetizing.

ALP.   But what is there left to discuss, Socrates? For you have heard all that I have to offer.

SOC.   Yet you have not, as it appears to me, convinced us that a man may be truly happy in this life, only that for so long as those desires are fulfilled and he retains the acquisitions of them, a man or woman may be said to be happy. But unhappiness follows when these are unfulfilled, or when the acquisitions are removed. What say you, Telamon, are you convinced upon this matter?

TEL.   I must confess, Socrates, that I am not at this moment; and I believe that Alphaeus has much left to say on this subject, and which I have heard him announce on many occasions.

SOC. Shall we then return to the point, Alphaeus, and will you answer to me some more of my questions? As it seems to me that there are few subjects upon which a man will require certainty, and that are more important than that which is before us.

ALP. I am happy to continue and convince you, remembering that my time is spoken for and is nearly at an end here.

SOC. Then I shall hasten like Phaeton on his morning ride.

ALP. That would be helpful, Socrates.

SOC. It would, indeed. Let us return, then, to the few desires you enumerated, and remember what they were. Will you repeat them for our benefit, Alphaeus.

ALP. I will, and they are the foundation of all happiness. In no order they are wealth, power, health, a good family and a fine reputation, in sufficient quantity to satisfy the ambition of each person.

SOC. And do you perceive any thing common to these five?

ALP. I do, in so far as they are all of them desires, and are capable of producing happiness by their fulfillment.

SOC. Is it, then, that the desire for wealth is the primary desire, or the desire for the happiness that such wealth may provide?

ALP. It makes no difference, Socrates, for it is known to all that wealth leads to happiness, and is the flower of its acquisition.

SOC. And is the case the same with the other desires you recalled?

ALP. It is, and definitely so.

SOC. What then do you say to the man or woman who approaches to death, and then realizes that all these things are to be left behind together with the shroud?

ALP. It is nearly the same case with us all, no matter how little one has to leave behind. He, then, will be happy who approaches death, knowing that what he has acquired will be passed on to others; and that their happiness is a gift of his. No man can hope for more than a happy life and a content death, and in this is true happiness, my friend.

SOC. This is a comfortable life you describe, Alphaeus, and is it one that is attained with ease?

68 *Release Thyself*

ALP. It varies according to the individual, and is easily attained by some but with no little effort by others.

SOC. And do you still maintain that what is common in these various desires, is that they *are* all desires, and are productive of happiness?

ALP. I do, if they are fulfilled.

SOC. And further, that happiness is the common object of these same desires?

ALP. It is.

SOC. Then, does it not appear to you that these desires, which produce happiness, desire that which they do not as yet possess, that is, happiness? Like an acorn germinating into a horse, or a man producing coins from an empty purse.

ALP. It is not unknown, Socrates, that two different things coming together, and uniting into a mixed compound, may produce a third thing, which is neither of the two taken separately.

SOC. Though not unknown, yet it may be said that of such compounds if one or the other of the elements is removed, the compound fails and will not be that third thing. And if we apply this to your happiness, if desire is removed then happiness fails; or if the object of desire is removed or not attained, then again it fails, as neither of these things contains happiness in itself, which is alone the result of their union. But, maybe it is that happiness can be achieved without desiring it, and may not be appreciated when it is present, yet is sorely missed when it is absent.

ALP. What a complicated web you weave, Socrates, in which to ensnare yourself. For, as I have already said, the desires are for the objects enumerated, and not for happiness as such; for what sane man desires happiness alone and not as the result of wealth and power and the others I have repeatedly described? You, Socrates, are not sure if you are happy, nor whether you can ever be truly happy in this life, and because of this you try to trap others in this same web; and your lack of desire for these things, or your inability to attain to them and fulfill whatever desires you may possess, distorts your judgment of happiness either when present to yourself, or so obviously enjoyed by others. Your envy goes before you like a watchman's lamp at night.

The Alphaeus 69

SOC. I cannot deny that I admire your certainty upon a matter of such great note; and in asking you to share this with me, and Telamon here, I had no intention or design to unsettle you or to provoke in you any disease. What then, Alphaeus, would you say that is in wealth, which is truly the object of desire?

ALP. What is this nonsense now? Wealth itself, simply and wholly, is the object of the desire for wealth.

SOC. And will this be the same respecting power?

ALP. Without any doubt it will.

SOC. And also with a fine reputation, and the other objects of desire you proposed?

ALP. Yes, these also, Socrates.

SOC. Then would you say that it is possible for a man or a woman to be truly happy who only possesses a necessary portion of wealth and power, and the others?

ALP. You tell me, Socrates, for your answer will be born from experience.

SOC. That is not a fair answer, nor even any answer, Alphaeus.

ALP. Then my answer is this, that such a man or woman will be happy in proportion to their actual possession of those things; and that a necessary portion for his continued existence will bestow a similar portion of happiness, sufficient, at least, to prevent death or suicide.

SOC. You speak of mathematical ratios, Alphaeus, as if happiness may be calculated from a formula, such as $h = d^3 \times f$, or something of the like. Is this what you propose to us, and to those that subscribe to your instructions?

ALP. I perceive your facetious undertone, Socrates, but it does not conceal the truth of what you say, inasmuch as the formula you have contrived is very near to being the case. For happiness is not, as you seem to experience, either an accident or the result of chance.

SOC. Then we should now examine this formula, or others of a similar nature, and reveal whether it is in truth infrangible.

ALP. And how do you propose that we should proceed in this examination, in a manner that will not exhaust our remaining time?

70   *Release Thyself*

SOC. In this way, Alphaeus, I suggest. Do you consider that a man may desire something, the acquisition of which will not be to his benefit, and may even prove to be a cause of detriment?

ALP. No man or woman, if their sanity is intact, would desire that which they know to be detrimental.

SOC. Then do you say that a sane man or woman desires only that which they know to be beneficial?

ALP. I do say that, certainly, Socrates.

SOC. And is this the case not only with sane men, but with powerful men also, and rulers and kings?

ALP. Even more so with these kinds of men.

SOC. But do you not recall that son of Gordius and the goddess, who, when his wish was granted, by his touch turned every thing to gold, and all but extinguished his own royal life?

ALP. I do so recall.

SOC. Do you also recall that Narcissus and his languorous death, and many others whose deep desires were fulfilled, or who perished for the lack of such fulfillment?

ALP. I do, Socrates, as I have been told these same tales and many others besides; but these, and the others, were blind desires in common, and not those of intelligent men.

SOC. But are not all desires blind, Alphaeus?

ALP. They are as blind as the man who possesses them.

SOC. Yet, as you said earlier, it is not knowledge that we are discussing but happiness; unless you say that the latter is dependent upon the former. Is this what you are now proposing?

ALP. The obvious needs no such proposition, as the knowledge of what is desirable is a common ground of man; but the intelligent man knows clearly what he desires and why.

SOC. Then are the desires of the ignorant the same as those of the intelligent, or do you say that they are different?

ALP. Come, Socrates, and cease your pedantry, as I began by saying that the desires I enumerated were those of all men and women, whether ignorant, intelligent or otherwise.

The Alphaeus 71

SOC. But you affirm that there are some who desire that which appears to be beneficial to them, but that when acquired then appears to be detrimental?

ALP. I do, as I qualified a similar answer earlier.

SOC. I remember your qualification, and it follows that an intelligent man or woman will know which objects of desire are beneficial and which are not. Is this then a position you will affirm?

ALP. I will and I do.

SOC. And do you say that there are some things, though desired, that are beneficial to one man yet detrimental to another?

ALP. I believe that there are such things, the results of the acquisition of which are affected by the condition of the acquirer.

SOC. But are there also some things that affect the condition of the acquirer himself, and not that of the acquired?

ALP. Again you repeat and state the obvious, Socrates, as the desire for most, if not all things, is not merely for acquisition's sake, but for the change in condition that these acquisitions will then enable.

SOC. And does it follow then, Alphaeus, that an intelligent man will not only know what things, as objects of desire, are beneficial, but also what beneficial changes in condition these same acquired objects will donate?

ALP. He will.

SOC. But the ignorant man will neither know what objects of desire are beneficial, nor what beneficial changes their acquisition will promote; or would you say otherwise?

ALP. I would not, as the case is fairly stated.

SOC. And is it likewise fairly stated that an intelligent man will also know how to retain and preserve his acquisitions, and the beneficial changes they have facilitated, but that an ignorant man will not?

ALP. Likewise.

SOC. And do you hold, Alphaeus, that this knowledge of what it is beneficial to desire, and the benefits its fulfillment will bestow, is essential for any man or woman who wishes to be truly happy?

ALP. Yes, Socrates, I do.

72 *Release Thyself*

SOC. Then we are close to the heart of this matter, and I would propose to you this further question.

ALP. And what is that question?

SOC. Whether you say that the desirable is the same with the good?

ALP. It is, to the intelligent man or woman.

SOC. But not, would you say, to the ignorant man or woman?

ALP. I would not.

SOC. Then, is it the case that to an ignorant man or woman, wealth, power, reputation and those others, may not be beneficial and good in their acquisition?

ALP. They may be, but they may also prove to be so many curses.

SOC. But, Alphaeus, those you teach, are they intelligent or ignorant men and women?

ALP. For the most part they are intelligent.

SOC. And thus, is it that they know what it is that is good to desire, and what is good in the desirable, and what the good will be resulting from such acquisitions? Or is this what you teach them?

ALP. They have a basic knowledge of these things, but it is my calling to develop that knowledge, and to teach how these very things can be known with certainty.

SOC. If, that is, they have already acquired sufficient wealth to supply your modest fees.

ALP. That is so.

SOC. Then the most important element of your teaching is that which concerns the nature of goodness, and the good, and how it is to be known with certainty, or would you say otherwise?

ALP. This is, essentially, what I teach.

SOC. And do you also teach what the nature of man consists of?

ALP. I am not an arrogant man, Socrates. Hence, I know my boundaries, and do not attempt to teach such a subject, leaving it to the intelligence of my pupils to decide upon.

SOC. But surely, Alphaeus, ignorance regarding either or both of these subjects will totally eclipse the intelligence of anything else?

The Alphaeus 73

ALP. What is this that you say now, Socrates?

SOC. Only this, that if a man does not know his own nature and what in reality he is, how can he know what is good for him in any and every sphere of his life? And further, if a man does not know what the good is, how can he know whether that which he desires is, or will be, beneficial? And how then can a man who is ignorant of both of these, know what is beneficial or good to others, whether or not they desire those things you described, or want them, or profess they must and should have them? For the danger is akin to feeding a bird with sand, or a hungry lion with bricks.

ALP. You speak now of things that all men know, save for those who are insane or not yet of age.

SOC. Though all men may know these things, good Alphaeus, there are few, if any, that can remember them.

ALP. Your arrogance announces itself like a Spartan horn, Socrates, designed by the few to strike fear in the hearts of the many. Unless you perceive the state of all men's minds, your words are just bluster and a loud but hollow judgment.

SOC. The horn you mention is a herald of dire times, whether blown by one or a multitude. But your position, as you describe it, is clear, and is this – that it is your part to develop the basic knowledge that men and women possess regarding the good and the desirable, and this to the point of certainty; and also, that you leave the knowledge of what the self of man is for your pupils to decide upon, according to their own intelligence. Are you content with this summation, Alphaeus?

ALP. It will do.

SOC. That is well; but you said further, that to an intelligent man or woman the good and the desirable are one and the same thing; is this again your judgment?

ALP. It is, and your repetition is becoming tedious.

SOC. Then we shall avoid it in our further discussion, if only you will answer me this.

ALP. And what would that be?

SOC. Whether you would say that all things desirable are then good?

74 *Release Thyself*

ALP. Again you repeat yourself, as I have already said that to an intelligent man they are.

SOC. Not quite, Alphaeus, but it matters little. So inasmuch as this is true, do you say that no man would desire that which he knows would be harmful to acquire?

ALP. I do.

SOC. But it is possible to desire something, through ignorance, which will indeed prove harmful when obtained?

ALP. That is indeed my considered opinion, Socrates.

SOC. And it is your part, as you have stated it, to teach what it is good to desire, and what is good in the desirable, but not to advance a knowledge of the desiring nature, leaving that to individual or common judgment.

ALP. Unlike yourself, I assume that all intelligent men and women know in what their nature consists.

SOC. I, too, predict that this will be the condition with all such truly intelligent souls.

ALP. Why must you continue so, Socrates, with this incessant slight of mouth, where you add words to mine as if they were insufficient? Thus your addition of *truly* to *intelligent* is ungracious and pedantic, and changes not the essence of what I said.

SOC. Then I withdraw that truly, Alphaeus, and leave your assumption as it was. Yet, from my own experience, there are many who desire to know in what their nature consists, and what it is to be a man or woman or soul. And there are many more who assume that they know what this self is, and seek happiness according to that assumption. But few men there are who know their essential nature, and they are to be found with great difficulty, being all but invisible to the many. In which do you camp yourself, Alphaeus, as one who desires this knowledge, or one who assumes he already has this knowledge, or one who possesses this knowledge in truth?

ALP. The third is mine, as the saying goes.

SOC. It is but a saying from a play, good man. But come now, let us then armed with your certain knowledge, and my desire for learning, approach to the truth of the question.

ALP. Let us do that, please.

The Alphaeus 75

SOC. Imagine, then, a man or a woman, who has all possible wealth and power and health, and the fulfillment of the desires you pronounced; and then imagine another one, who has but a necessary portion of the same, in order to maintain existence. Which of these do you consider will be the happiest?

ALP. I have heard that this is a question that you love to banter around, Socrates; but I will not give you the answer I know you have stored up, and which you know that I know. My answer is simple, and it is the man or woman who has fulfilled those desires that will be the happiest – and tell me not that it is whichever of them is the wisest. For a wise man would never be poor.

SOC. Then are all poor people unwise and ignorant?

ALP. They are.

SOC. And likewise wanting in power, and health and good family and reputation?

ALP. Undoubtedly so.

SOC. Must they all then be likewise unhappy?

ALP. They must.

SOC. Does it follow that all wealthy people are then wise?

ALP. It does, Socrates, it does; as their wealth is the fruit of a wise use of life.

SOC. And, therefore, they are happy?

ALP. They are.

SOC. And does it then follow that all poor people are most unhappy?

ALP. It does, as I have already said.

SOC. So, this unhappiness that the poor suffer, is this the product then of unfulfilled desires, such as those you have espoused?

ALP. It is, and very much so.

SOC. But I see before us a puzzling equation, which has been trying to voice itself throughout our investigation.

ALP. I am not surprised, Socrates; but go on then, give it some air if you so wish.

76 *Release Thyself*

SOC. Thank you, my friend, and I will, as I suspect that it is veiled behind your own assertions, given with such alacrity.

ALP. Proceed.

SOC. Does it, then, equate that those who have fulfilled the most of their desires therefore, being happy, acquire a greater portion of good to themselves? And that those who have fulfilled only a necessary portion of the desires you hold, thereby acquire or continue to enjoy only a necessary portion of good? Is this an equation you would assent to as being accurate?

ALP. I would, Socrates, as far as it goes.

SOC. Then the wealthy, the healthy, the renowned, the well-born and the powerful are all of them good?

ALP. They are, and also they are happy.

SOC. And the poor, the infirm, the unknown, the lowly born and the singular are all of them not good?

ALP. They may be good to a certain degree, but it is an impotent good.

SOC. And do you say further that this same ratio can be applied to wisdom? So that the poor and those others are also unwise, and that the wealthy and their fellows are wise?

ALP. I do so say, and repeat.

SOC. But what of beauty; is it the same process with this?

ALP. It is.

SOC. So that the poor and the others are not beautiful, but the wealthy and the desire-fulfilled are?

ALP. That is the case I support and have observed.

SOC. In summing up, my friend, your argument, it is that all poor people and those others are not only unhappy, but likewise they are evil, ignorant, ugly and impotent. And that all wealthy people, and the others, are happy, good, wise and beautiful.

ALP. That is, Socrates, my argument.

SOC. What then, Alphaeus, if a man or a woman, poor from birth, on a sudden acquires very substantial wealth; does this same person, on a sudden, also acquire substantial happiness?

ALP. They do.

SOC. And this together with goodness and wisdom and beauty?

ALP. You are trying to entrap me, Socrates.

SOC. But no, Alphaeus, as you have already entrapped yourself. Yet answer the question, whether the sudden acquisition of abundant wealth, or power, or health, or fame, likewise bestows the equally sudden abundance of goodness, happiness, beauty and wisdom, and other such excellences.

ALP. Enough of this, Socrates; I have patronized your argument from respect to Telamon, when I would have left some time ago if alone. You talk of extremes and exceptions and miss the normal and the common, to which I look in assessing any person.

SOC. Yet, good man, if you do not answer this question, both Telamon here and I, and in truth all who ask such questions, will know not where to turn, or who to ask, if those such as you refuse the opportunity to answer upon subjects about which you are certain.

ALP. Then I will answer, in recognition of my good friend here, that such a sudden acquisition and fulfillment of desires would at the least provide the opportunity for the acquisition of such goodness, wisdom and beauty as you propose.

SOC. Thank you, and I believe that there is one last question which should seal the circle, so to speak, and reveal to us the heart of the matter.

ALP. Then ask it, Socrates, and do not delay, as my time here is now getting short.

SOC. It is simple, and it is this; would the sudden removal of wealth and health and those other fulfilled desires you champion, cause the sudden removal also of happiness, and goodness, wisdom and beauty? Consider this, Alphaeus, and whether you believe it to be true.

ALP. (*standing up in silence for long moments*) Talk not to me of belief, man, for knowledge is my calling, not belief!

SOC. There are many of the present time, and there will be many more in the future, who profess to know certain things, having been schooled in the ways of detailed convincement and thesis; yet at the same time do not believe what they speak of, or write about, or claim to know. So, in deference to you, Alphaeus, I will alter the question this way: do you then know this to be true?

ALP. By the dog, how you infuriate me! I will co-operate no more with your semantic gymnastics, Socrates, as you are plainly involved only with your own self-justification and defence for a way of life that you are trapped in, by your own lack of practical wisdom. You are an idiot and full with mania, and see not that those theoretic virtues you embrace so much are of *no* worth at all to those who have not fulfilled the desires I have strenuously and exhaustingly explained. I condemn you as a hack, as you will soon be condemned as a conjuror. Come, Telamon, we are leaving this place!

(Telamon then raises himself to one knee, and looks into the eyes of Socrates, who bows his head slowly.)

TEL. I think not, Alphaeus, for I cannot leave with these conflicting thoughts racing in me unresolved.

ALP. But they are resolved, Telamon, they are! The doubts have been sown by Socrates here, and they are *his* doubts, not yours, and certainly they are not mine.

TEL. But I own them to be mine now, my friend.

ALP. Then I must leave you both with them like some ill-disciplined nursery, as I am due in the court of Alampis in but a little time. Farewell, until later, Telamon; and good-bye, Socrates.

TEL. Farewell.

(Alphaeus departs. Socrates is silent, his head still bowed low and deep in thought.)

TEL. Socrates, my friend, why do you sit so? Are you troubled by what we have just heard?

SOC. *(after a long pause)* No, good Telamon, I am not; and I sit here so because of a voice I seem to hear and that prompts me to be quiet, to be still and to see.

TEL. Is, then, our conversation over, and would you rather that I retired now with Alphaeus?

SOC. This, our conversation, concerns a subject of greatest moment, and not the one that appears now as obvious.

TEL. What subject do you mean, and how is it not obvious?

SOC. It has been standing in front of us, like some doe blending in with its surroundings, and is only obvious and visible to a hunter.

TEL. Is it the nature of happiness that you see, and which is blended with the confusions we have heard?

SOC. It is, and barely behind it I survey its sire. Do you wish to pursue this, with all the stealth and guile that we can muster?

TEL. I do so very much, and follow you.

SOC. By the huntress then, Telamon my friend, let us hunt, and together with her close upon our prey.

TEL. Only lead and show me the tracks.

SOC. What think you of the happiness promoted just now?

TEL. I almost think the opposite to that which I have held for years.

SOC. And what is this opposite that you now hold close?

TEL. That true happiness cannot be generated from the fulfillment of those desires which we lately considered; and that far from being satiable and dignified they appear to be boundless and base on their own, leading only to a form of happiness both temporary and contingent.

SOC. What then, do you perceive other desires not lately mentioned, that admit of some bound and more worth?

TEL. No, I do not perceive them, but suspect that they must exist, for those so recently described now appear to be insufficient for the purpose of attaining true happiness.

SOC. Yet, Telamon, those desires so well pronounced just now, may not be as boundless or base as they presently appear to you; but that they are just the trees that obscure our prey, and if we look well to them, and to that, they will reveal even more than they obscure, and we will see the difference clearly.

TEL. Say on, Socrates.

SOC. Do you not remember the rumour from those celebrations, of which I know you were an auditor in your young manhood – that from the bosom of the mother of life are two great fountains formed, being the one of soul and the other of virtue?

TEL. I hear, and now remember, as if waking from a nocturnal dream.

SOC. And that from those ample fountains all souls and all virtues are nourished.

TEL. I hear it again, yet anew.

80 *Release Thyself*

SOC. So that each is nourished from both, as to be nurtured together, being for the one the life and for the other the excellence.

TEL. It is indeed so said and is a mystery.

SOC. It is. Then let us continue to hunt, my good friend, with the truth of her mystery before us.

TEL. Please, Socrates, continue, and I am very much with you now.

(As Socrates is preparing to speak, a woman appears as if from nowhere. She is tall but bent, and at the dawn of old age; she wears her ragged dress with dignity, her feet are bare, and she is carrying a basket on her back containing many bundles of twigs and herbs. When she smiles in greeting, her blue eyes sparkle and her face appears old and yet young.)

WOMAN Good morning, gentlemen, and I apologise for interrupting your conversation, but I need to rest for a few moments beneath this fine tree, and to share your shade if you will allow. I shall be gone from you very shortly.

TEL. Please, lady, join us and let me help you with the burden that you bear.

WOMAN It is no burden, young man, merely some necessities of life; but thank you, and I shall sit for just a little time.

TEL. You are welcome.

WOMAN This is a beautiful place to rest and to contemplate the power of that temple. Is that where you have been this day?

TEL. No, lady, it is not. My friend here and I met by accident, as I was walking to the court of Alampis.

WOMAN *(laughing)* I do not think that anyone meets your friend by accident, and it is sure that he must have come to this place for some good reason or other.

TEL. You speak as if one who knows him.

WOMAN I do not know him personally, yet I do know his name, as do many who walk invisible through this city.

TEL. What can you mean by that, to walk invisible through this city?

WOMAN Good Socrates, if I may address you so, have you ever seen me before this day?

SOC. Welcome, lady, but I do not think that I have.

WOMAN And yet I have seen you many times as you walk the streets of Athena's city, and I have heard you, and have even stood close by to you on not a few occasions. This is what it is to be invisible.

SOC. And would you say, good woman, that you have seen me and heard me talk, and even stood close to me however many times, by accident or was it by design?

WOMAN I must admit that it was and is by my design.

SOC. What, then, is your purpose behind such a design?

WOMAN To listen to you, and to hear you, as well as those with whom you converse.

SOC. Then you will be aware of some of my conversations, and how well or otherwise they have been received.

WOMAN I am aware, Socrates.

SOC. So what think you of them, lady?

WOMAN I think they are the conversations of a good man, however well or ill they are received.

SOC. I pray that is the truth; but do you wish to know what it was that my friend Telamon here and I, and one other who lately departed, were discussing?

WOMAN I do, as I saw that other as I approached, and there was hardly a pebble across his path that did not receive from him a most vehement kick.

TEL. He is a passionate man.

WOMAN Aye, he is and he looked deeply troubled.

SOC. And it is a passionate subject to many, for we were enquiring as to whether it is possible to be truly happy in this life.

WOMAN Your departing friend seemed not to be so.

TEL. Please, be not quick with your judgment, for he was angry and short of time.

WOMAN I do not judge him, sir, I only report what I saw, and those pebbles had done him no harm.

TEL. (*laughing*) Yes, he did not seem too happy with our talk.

82 *Release Thyself*

SOC. Good lady, what would be your answer to that same simple question; do you think that it is possible to be truly happy in this life?

WOMAN I can only answer that, Socrates, from the experience of my life, and it will much depend upon how such happiness is defined.

TEL. It is certain, Socrates, that this lady has heard you often, as now she now questions just like you. But come, good woman, would you say that you are happy?

WOMAN I am.

TEL. And has your happiness been achieved from the fulfillment of your desires?

WOMAN What know you of my desires, young man?

TEL. Please, I shall express my question another way. Would you say that your desires for wealth, health, power, reputation and good family have been fulfilled?

WOMAN (*laughing*) No, good fellow, they have not.

TEL. And yet you say that you are happy?

WOMAN I do.

TEL. Yet, according to my friend, the fulfillment of those desires is what happiness truly is, and therefore, by that mark, you cannot then be happy.

WOMAN It will not be your friend Socrates here who has said these things, so it must have been that other angry one; and he has made two towering assumptions, which are always a cause of error.

TEL. What assumptions are they, good lady?

WOMAN The first is that I even possess those named desires for such objects.

TEL. But do you not?

WOMAN I do not, and hence they will not be fulfilled.

TEL. And what was the second assumption that has caused or has lead to some error?

WOMAN It is that happiness may be measured and defined by such fulfillment of those same desires.

The Alphaeus 83

TEL. But, do you say that these desires are not common to all men and women?

WOMAN The desires may well be common but their objects, I think, are not.

TEL. Please, lady, explain your meaning to us.

WOMAN Have you not observed the attraction young children suffer for bright and sparkling things?

TEL. I have.

WOMAN And at times that attraction is so potent as to cause a crawling tot to lift itself up, or a walking tot to climb, as being focused solely upon the object of its desire, no risk or difficulty preventing. Have you observed this too, young man?

TEL. This, too, I have seen.

WOMAN And when that sparkling object is finally grasped, and held close to and examined, is the child then happy and fulfilled?

TEL. For a time it so appears.

WOMAN But what, then, if a brighter and more glittering object attracts the attention of that little person, is not the first put aside and the desire for it replaced?

TEL. It is.

WOMAN What say you of this form of happiness, good man, is it true?

TEL. I can only think that it is true for so long as it lasts.

WOMAN But when the happiness has departed what then happens to its truth?

TEL. It must surely depart along with it.

WOMAN Then the sparkling object itself was not sufficient to a permanent happiness.

TEL. It was not.

WOMAN Why so, young man; is that not now the question you should answer?

TEL. (*Quietly, after a long silent pause*) Because it was itself impermanent, and whether cast aside, lost, or when perished through time, it would depart and cease to be an object of desire.

84 *Release Thyself*

WOMAN (*Standing up*) For that very reason I am not happy from such fulfillment of the desires your friend announced, as it is as temporary as it is true, and, likewise, the form of happiness it promotes. But my time here is now over and there is another I must attend to, so farewell, good Telamon, and you dear Socrates; until another time when we may meet. And use such time well, both of you, as this life may be so very short.

TEL. Thank you, fair lady.

SOC. Woman, you are a blessing.

(*The woman departs, and is soon hidden among the ripening olive groves.*)

TEL. What kind of a woman was that, Socrates, and do you know who she is?

SOC. I do not know who she is, Telamon, but from her words, her bearing and presence she is most singular. Yet, from her clothing, her condition and her burden, she appears like many of the poor folk of our city, and is, as she said, all but invisible. She is not how she appears, I am sure.

TEL. And what she said concerning happiness seemed to strike at the heart of the argument we lately entertained, and which now seems so childish and trite.

SOC. Whatever else she is, she is a daughter of the huntress, or of that lady whose name this city bears. Yet come, Telamon, and let us finish what we started, with the assistance of that good woman beside us.

TEL. Then I will say what came to mind as I pondered upon her questions, and which seemed so clear as I listened to her voice.

SOC. Please continue, if you can.

TEL. It appeared to me, Socrates, that if the object of desire is impermanent, then any happiness resulting from its acquisition will be impermanent likewise. And, further, that those very desires, in themselves, are desiring something permanent and real, but which they do not know, being for the most part allowed to wander in the dark. Yet what those stable things are that they truly feel around for, I cannot ascertain or yet perceive.

SOC. And what is it, Telamon, which allows these desires to wander around in the dark, feeling for something to fulfill them?

TEL. I have to think it can only be us, the very man or woman.

The Alphaeus 85

SOC. In the name of heaven, then, why should this be, that they are released to wander so blindly?

TEL. Do you mean, why are they not directed to some more certain or permanent ends?

SOC. That is indeed what I mean.

TEL. Can it be because the man or woman involved does not see or know either what these certain or permanent ends are, to which these their desires are fumbling?

SOC. Be careful here, my friend, that you do not divide these very desires from the man or woman who possesses them. For they are not separate like so many pets or children, but are yet an element in the nature of man.

TEL. It must be, then, if the man is ignorant of what it is good to desire then his desires are blind likewise, and will move the man towards whatever appears to be desirable and good.

SOC. Further to this, Telamon, you, who are a student of happiness, have heard it said that the knowledge of what man is will be well left to the discernment of each individual; is this not so?

TEL. It is.

SOC. And have you not heard also, even today, that there are those who sell the knowledge of what it is good to desire, what is good in the desirable, and what good will ensue from the fulfillment of desire?

TEL. I have indeed heard this too, and many times over.

SOC. Yet if there is poor knowledge or wrong knowledge of the desiring nature, how can it happen that a man can know accurately what is good for him, whether it is desired or otherwise?

TEL. I do not think that he can.

SOC. And what will then happen if a man has poor knowledge or wrong knowledge of what the good is; can he approach with any certainty and confidence to that which he desires as being good?

TEL. Again, he can not.

SOC. But is it possible, my friend, for a man to possess no idea whatever of what the good truly is?

TEL. I am not sure what you mean by this question.

86 Release Thyself

SOC. It is simple, Telamon, and thus; if a man has no idea whatever of what the good is, would he ever be drawn towards or desire that which appears to be good?

TEL. He would not, as it would not even appear to be desirable to him.

SOC. Come then, and let us hunt down our prey, as now it appears very close. Shall we, then, after all this energy, attempt to define what desire truly is?

TEL. Please, Socrates, it is necessary.

SOC. Does not, then, desire desire something?

TEL. It does.

SOC. And is that something, in the first place, desired for the desiring nature?

TEL. It is.

SOC. And would the desiring nature desire that which would be harmful to itself?

TEL. It would not.

SOC. Then the desiring nature desires only that which will be good or beneficial to itself; is this what you would affirm?

TEL. I would and I do.

SOC. Then is desire itself, in all things that are capable of possessing it, the power that moves those same things towards their good, and toward nothing else?

TEL. I think very much now that this is what it is.

SOC. And do you think that for each thing there is a good that is proper to it, such as with a plant or an animal, of whatever types they may be?

TEL. I think that there must be.

SOC. And will it be to this proper good that the desiring nature is moved, as being the most appropriate and best of all goods?

TEL. It will be, and very much so.

SOC. And this whether or not that same nature is conscious of its own proper good?

TEL. How can it be otherwise, Socrates? All the flora and fauna of nature lives so, and is moved in the way you have described.

The Alphaeus 87

SOC. And maybe even nature herself, Telamon, and the body of the whole universe she inspires.

TEL. That is a most profound thought, Socrates.

SOC. But does appear to you to be a true one?

TEL. It does.

SOC. What then, is man so very different from the rest of the universe, in that he has not his own proper good?

TEL. He would seem to be different in one important manner.

SOC. And what is this difference, my friend?

TEL. It is this: for mankind alone seems not to know in what his proper good really consists.

SOC. This may well be true, Telamon, but does it prevent mankind from yet desiring it?

TEL. It does not.

SOC. So that a man, knowing not what his proper good is, notwithstanding will he still desire it?

TEL. He will.

SOC. Will then all his various desires be aimed at, though not accurately, the acquisition of his own proper good?

TEL. Surely, they will.

SOC. And will not that good which is the proper good of the species invariably be the good of individuals?

TEL. It certainly will, without a doubt.

SOC. Then does it appear to you that there is a proper good for mankind, which will comprehend the good of every and each man and woman?

TEL. It appears so very much at this moment.

SOC. And does it also appear to you that the realization of this good would thus produce the best of life for man, both generally and in particular?

TEL. I cannot see that it could be otherwise.

88 *Release Thyself*

SOC. Then, what say you now of the desires we lately heard, and which you have heard described so very often; are they then the desire for some proper good or goods, though the aim be not accurate or true?

TEL. What is it that you mean, Socrates?

SOC. Do you still affirm that the various desires of things are of the power that moves them towards good?

TEL. I do.

SOC. And do you affirm also that, for whatever reason, it is possible for a man or woman to desire their proper good, but yet be mistaken in their belief that the desired object will provide it or even is it?

TEL. Again, I do, and very much so.

SOC. Then let us look once more to those desires your friend announced, or, more accurately, to those objects of desire, and see if we can now uncover their truth.

TEL. Please proceed, Socrates.

SOC. This mighty desire for wealth, then, which is suffered by so many men and women; what is it, do you think, that its acquisition will enable them to do?

TEL. Anything, and everything at all.

SOC. But, Telamon, is it possible for a man to do everything merely from the acquisition of wealth?

TEL. It may not be possible, but it may yet be desired.

SOC. Then of this everything that wealth enables the doing of, can any of it be done successfully without the knowledge of how best to do it?

TEL. I do not think that it can.

SOC. And without this knowledge of how best to do anything, would not chaos and disappointment ensue?

TEL. It would.

SOC. And yet with this knowledge of how it is best to do anything, would not the results of this be the best likewise?

TEL. They would.

SOC. But what, then, Telamon, can the knowledge of how it is best to do anything and everything at all, in every sphere of life, or even in the

The Alphaeus 89

living of life itself, be the result of the acquisition of wealth, no matter how vast or inexhaustible?

TEL. No, Socrates, I cannot see how it can.

SOC. What then would you name that virtue or excellence which would enable any man or woman to do what is best in any and every circumstance, and to lead the best life, and to be the best possible at all?

TEL. Surely, Socrates, its name must be wisdom.

SOC. And would this wisdom enable its possessor to do whatever he or she does in the best possible manner, and to do everything good and well?

TEL. It would.

SOC. Then do you think that a life such as that, the life of wisdom, would be a happy one?

TEL. I do and very much so.

SOC. And would you say that it is happy because it is good, or that it is good because it is happy?

TEL. It must be that it is happy because it is good.

SOC. Then the knowledge of and the acquisition of good is the way to fulfillment and happiness.

TEL. It is certain.

SOC. And this knowledge of the good, can it be obtained otherwise than through being wise?

TEL. It can not.

SOC. Is this not then true wealth, Telamon, to know the good, to live it, to be it, and to enjoy the lasting happiness that it radiates?

TEL. It is indeed true wealth, Socrates, and to be treasured and shared more than any other.

SOC. Then does it appear to you, that the desire for wealth in mankind is but the result of that deeper longing for wisdom, and for the great good and the happiness that it involves?

TEL. It does appear to be so now, Socrates; and even further, that this wealth is believed to provide security, which only wisdom can truly provide. Hence, the popular desire for wealth is but the unconscious

90 *Release Thyself*

desire of the soul for wisdom expressing itself, and this is as clear to me now as a brilliant sunrise.

SOC. You are inspired by some goddess, my friend.

TEL. It seems that this whole place is inspired at this moment.

SOC. So come, let us breathe it in. *(after a pause)* Do you think, Telamon, that the case may be similar with the other objects of desire that our friend pronounced; and that they, too, are the result of the deeper and less conscious desire of the soul for some excellence or virtue?

TEL. I can hardly think now that it could be otherwise.

SOC. Shall we then look at them, without prolixity, and see if this is truly the case?

TEL. That would indeed be good.

SOC. What, then, of power, which is so much desired by so many; is it not the desire to prevent any and every incursion of harm, and the facility to do anything without boundary or fear of failure?

TEL. I think very much that this is what is perceived as power, and is then so desired.

SOC. And yet, are these not the primary marks of fortitude and courage?

TEL. They are.

SOC. Then does it appear that this popular desire for power is but the result of a deeper desire of the soul for real fortitude and courage?

TEL. It does, and wonderfully so.

SOC. And what of the desire for good health? Is it not the desire to be fit, and well, and to be able to bring all extremes under some control or bound?

TEL. It is.

SOC. And are these not the marks of temperance, and that virtue which bounds the infinite power of extension?

TEL. They are.

SOC. Then, again, does it appear that this common desire for good health is but the result of that deeper desire of the soul for temperance and self-control and preservation?

The Alphaeus 91

TEL. It does so appear now, clearly.

SOC. What then of fine reputation, Telamon; can you perceive of what deep longing this is the result?

TEL. I believe now that I can.

SOC. So bring it to light, my friend.

TEL. It appears to me that a fine reputation is desired because it bestows an image of how a man wishes to appear; and that when that reputation is challenged a sense of injustice ensues, which in turn leads to anger. Hence, Socrates, I say that the desire for a fine reputation is the result of the deeper desire of the soul for justice, both in the giving and the receiving, and even in the being just. For, if that is truly the virtue of the man, it can never be changed by erroneous assault or rumour.

SOC. I cannot but agree with you, Telamon. Yet there is one more object of desire, at least, of those that were enumerated by Alphaeus; and that is the desire for a good family. And it appears to me that this is the least difficult of them all, and what deep longing of the soul that it indicates and is born from.

TEL. Please, then, say what it is, Socrates.

SOC. Union, Telamon, it is union; and it is the virtue of that which is most simple in us, and which enables us to be at one with ourselves, with those around us, with the world of man and nature, and with the universe itself and all the Gods from which it *is*. This is the best of all families, which our souls desire to have and to be a part of, as it is the excellence of that which is the best in us.

TEL. That is truly remarkable, Socrates, and is indeed the very best of families and the most beautiful virtue.

SOC. It is, and there are many others that are indicated by the objects of desire to mankind; but they must wait until another time. Yet see, Telamaon, our prey is now in front of us, and rather than pierce we should embrace it.

TEL. Please, let us do that, my dear friend.

SOC. We have seen, then, that the acquisition of wealth, power, reputation, health and good family do not of themselves lead to lasting happiness, have we not?

TEL. That we have.

SOC. But that these are merely substitutes for those real goods the soul seeks, which are, among others, wisdom, fortitude, temperance, justice and union. Can we imagine that the life of such virtues can be any thing else but happy and fulfilling?

TEL. I, for one, can not.

SOC. Then in as much as these virtues are the true goods of the soul, so a life in their possession will not only be the best, but also truly the happiest; and if it is possible to be truly happy in this life, or in the many lives to come, it can only be from the possession and expression of virtue, which is the true excellence and good of each and every thing. For what a thing truly becomes, that it can never lose.

TEL. By the heavens, Socrates, it now appears so obvious. But, finally, do you think that it is indeed possible to be truly happy in this life?

SOC. I believe, good Telamon, that it may not be impossible.

(At this moment, Alphaeus appears from behind a tree, where he has been standing for a time and listening.)

ALP. Forgive me, Socrates, and you, Telamon, for thus interrupting your conversation.

TEL. Alphaeus, my friend, you are welcome, and the conversation, I think, has now come near to some end.

ALP. I fear that it is so, and that I have missed it.

TEL. But how come you here at this time? Was there some problem or delay at the court of Alampis, where you were due to be speaking even now?

ALP. There is indeed a delay there now, as I did not reach even near to the gates, and those gathered will be wondering where I am.

TEL. Why then are you not there, Alphaeus?

ALP. Because some astonishing event occurred, and which has compelled me to come back here to you both.

SOC. Please, Alphaeus, sit with us, and tell us what event has so astonished you.

TEL. Yes, please sit, as you look both exhausted and perplexed.

ALP. That I am; yet I shall tell you what has happened, and then you may decide whether to comply with my request or not.

The Alphaeus 93

TEL. Then speak, Alphaeus, and we will listen.

ALP. I left you both at a pace I know you saw, and not at all pleased with the discussion and how I had conducted myself. At no long distance from here I sat down beneath a fine broad tree, to try to collect my thoughts and emotions, and to understand why I had reacted in the manner I did. I do not know how long I sat there considering these things, but when I looked up I saw a woman walking along the path in my direction. She was bent over from the weight of the basket she was carrying, and her clothes were ragged yet clean, and her feet were bare; her silver hair seemed to shine like the light of the moon, and it was this that induced me to observe her. When she came opposite and near to me she stopped, and unburdened herself of her load, and stood up straight. Her form, in truth, was most handsome, with hardly any resemblance to the bent figure I had seen only moments before. But then she turned her head and looked at me, and smiled, and, in the name of love, I swear that I have never seen such a happy smile before, nor eyes that glittered so brightly and so clearly. I stood up to greet her, and in that moment she collapsed with the slowness of a gently setting sun, and lay on the ground motionless. I rushed directly to her and laid her head upon my lap, trying my best to revive her. Then again she looked at me or even in me, and I perceived a radiance in her face that I had not thought humanly possible. I asked her what I could do to help her, but her reply arrested my very heart, for she said, "You can do nothing for me, young man, but there is something you must do for yourself."

"What is it that I must do?" I asked.

"On your soul you must promise that you will do it, as being the wish of one who is departing from you." she whispered.

"I will, I promise, if it is at all within my power." I answered, for at that moment I was convinced that there was nothing I would not do to serve this extraordinary woman.

"It is only in your power, Alphaeus." she said, and at the mention of my name from her voice, I felt tears form in my eyes, as if somehow I recognized the woman.

"What must I do, my lady?" I asked urgently.

"You must go back from whence you came and then finish what you have begun."

"But, where have I come from, and what did I begin?"

94 *Release Thyself*

"Go back, Alphaeus, to Socrates and to Telamon, or your search for happiness will be over."

"But, but I *am happy.*" I stuttered; yet as I said these words I knew then they were a lie, and the tears flowed from my eyes with no control.

"Go back, dear Alphaeus, for good." she sighed.

And as she said these words her eyes closed slowly, and her breath expired, and she lay there like one dead before me. I placed her head gently down upon the path, and stood up. I held my face close for many and long moments, totally moved by the whole experience, and unsure what to do about the dear woman's body. I uncovered my eyes slowly and turned to look upon her once more, but in the name of our lady she had gone. I paced in each direction trying to see her or her trace, but there was not a sign of her at all, nor of the basket she had been carrying. I then felt an elation that I have never felt before, a truly real and deeply happy elation. So by the wish of that divine woman, and by my own now eager will, I am back with you, my friends, for good.

*

*   *   *

THE PLATON

A DIALOGUE

ON SOUL

THE

PLATON

PERSONS OF THE DIALOGUE:

SOCRATES　　　PLATO

A VISITOR

SCENE: The prison cell of Socrates, the day before he is destined to suffer the cup of hemlock. Socrates has requested that his other friends, family and disciples do not attend him on this afternoon, so that this time may be shared only with Plato.

PLA. I see now very clearly why of necessity this must be so, and I am deeply grateful for your inspiring and timely explanation.

SOC. Then for this day that is truly sufficient. But, dear Plato, you wear a heavy and concerned frown, what troubles you so much that your very smile is now eclipsed?

PLA. Please, master, you know what troubles me so.

SOC. Aristocles, divine friend, why do you hold back, speak your mind now, if ever.

PLA. Then I will declare myself, though in doing so it may well reveal my flaws and immaturity.

SOC. Say nothing that will hurt yourself unless it is the truth – for your flaws are not unique, and your immaturity, as you name it, is only natural when compared to that which we have just now examined; and my own condition is not dissimilar when I make that same comparison.

PLA. Socrates, my father, hear then my concerns. I am very deeply troubled by your imminent departure from this life, and even more so from the causes that have brought about this unjust and vile sentence. I

98 *Release Thyself*

predict that I will be unable, no, that I shall be unwilling to stay in this city if such a great injustice is enacted. For the anger I experience at present will be but little when compared to that which I know will consume me on that fateful day, together with a sadness that will deluge me. It is as if I am watching an ignorant foolish parent killing their first and best offspring, for no other reason than that of attempting to speak the truth, which that parent then despises and exacts the ultimate penalty. *How, in the name of all that is good, can man be sunk so low?* When you go so shall I, and I may not ever return, as even the anticipation of such a loss is a pain I can barely endure.

SOC. Anger is the armour of young men, Plato, so do not believe that it is wrong in such a circumstance. But when your anger transforms itself into a certain focus, I know you will return here, drawn by the lady herself for her own divine and good purpose, and of which we have spoken before, inspired by that prediction of the oracle. Injustice is the offspring of ignorance and fear, as ever it was and will be. Though it appears to wield great power, injustice is truly impotent over virtue and its possessor, and is indeed its very own worst enemy. Remember this, dearest friend, for whether now, or in the next days, or in some time to come, depart I must, and it is only the manner in which I do so that should concern me, or you, or any who may know or hear of it. These men merely release me, and for that I bear no blame. It is they who shall be troubled in the future; and you, my fine friend, will continue what you have started, when you have learned all that you need to, and return here.

PLA. But what I need to learn I would have done so from you, yet now these men, as you call them, have denied me and others such a time with you.

SOC. That may be true; yet there is still time, Plato, we have this day and the next.

PLA. We have this afternoon, Socrates, but not the one that follows; that is for you and for those others whom we know.

SOC. What is it that you mean by this, dear friend?

PLA. If the prediction is accurate you will depart from us tomorrow.

SOC. That is so.

PLA. Then, by the love that is in me and is me, Socrates, I will not be a witness to it. I would not allow that servant to pass you the dark cup and not prevent him from performing such a dire act. I cannot be there at the end, Socrates, and will not watch you die!

SOC. (*after a pause*) I commend your open honesty, young man, and I would not want that servant to be subjected to more distress than he is so obviously experiencing at present. Be at peace, Plato, both with yourself and then with me, for death is but a word for a change that moves us all, and it will be this body of mine that suffers it, not me. But I know that you will be here, wherever you are, and as I leave I will say for you a prayer.

PLA. As I will for you, good master.

SOC. But come, my broad friend, let us enjoy what time remains, before that servant announces that some others have arrived.

PLA. I shall take my leave before they do so, as I have no wish to converse with anyone but you on this day.

SOC. Then let us converse, Plato, for I perceive that there is some other thing that troubles you at this time.

PLA. There is.

SOC. Speak, then, and clearly.

PLA. I will be as lucid as I am able, in attempting to express something which has been growing in importance for me, as my time with you has evolved. The question I am trying to form concerns the nature of soul; not only of that soul which ranks as the first and most total, but that in which the self of man truly consists. For, if I can be even more clear, the fact that man *is* and that he has soul is a condition I readily accept and assent to; but *why* he is, and why the human soul is necessary in the cosmic panorama, I have yet to discover a satisfactory reason for, and it involves completely what the purpose of such a being is, to this and in this beautiful order.

SOC. (*laughing*) It is good to know that your humour has not left you entirely, even at this late hour, for you bring now to our attention the happy heart of the matter, which has very much concerned us during our many long hours and days together. No, Plato, I am not making jest with you, and allow me some amusement at your timely mention of this most serious question of all.

100 *Release Thyself*

PLA. I think you will have predicted already that I would thus raise this profound matter.

SOC. You are not wrong, dear man, and such matters as these are well left until the last. What then shall we do? For the purpose of whatever soul we possess is intimately allied to that of the soul of all.

PLA. In truth this must be so.

SOC. Then must it not follow also, that the necessity for this soul, together with its energy and essence, will reveal much of its total nature?

PLA. This must indeed follow.

SOC. And that whatever necessity, energy and essence our souls possess, will likewise be related to, and dependent upon, that first and total soul?

PLA. Very true, Socrates.

SOC. How, then, shall we approach to this mystery, which is celebrated so much in secret places? Should we examine it as those who have already assumed that these souls, and other such similar natures, possess some real existence; or shall we, looking to other times, assume nothing of them, and examine them now anew?

PLA. I readily perceive that in some time to come there may be a great many who will deny the very existence of soul, both total and particular; and, in so doing, will be at such a loss for the reasons of any and all things, that only the desires surrounding these bodies will remain for them to enjoy, with nothing before and even less to come after this fleeting existence. Let us assume as little as we can, and begin from the beginning, as it is said.

SOC. (*after a pause*) Then with the assistance of some one of the Gods who cares for those who hunt these things, let us pray and make such a beginning.

PLA. I unite with such a prayer, and I am ready and with you, Socrates.

SOC. Are you willing, then, for this present purpose, to take the part of that man who assumes nothing of these things, and seeks only to come to truth?

PLA. I am happy so to do.

SOC. We will make this beginning then, good man. Let us divide the universe in this way.

PLA. In what way, Socrates?

SOC. The division is simple, and it is into those things that are and those things that are not.

PLA. That is indeed simple; and will you define in a simple manner these two types of things?

SOC. I conceive those things that *are* to be such as exist according to nature, and those things that *are not* to be such as have only an imagined or artificial existence.

PLA. I readily assent to this division.

SOC. And do you assent to this also, regarding those things that are not, that it is true that they are not?

PLA. I do.

SOC. And, likewise, regarding those things that are, that it is true that they are?

PLA. Again, I do.

SOC. And yet, my friend, is it possible that those things that are not can be known in any manner?

PLA. It is possible by whatever gnostic energy is capable of contacting such things, even the senses or the phantasy.

SOC. Then these things which are not cannot be said not to be always, but only that they sometimes are and sometimes are not. Is this a reasonable statement?

PLA. It is.

SOC. For, I divine, those things that never are can never be known in any manner, or would you say otherwise?

PLA. I would not, as even to imagine something that forever is not will prove to be impossible.

SOC. Would you say, then, that these things that sometimes exist may sometimes be known?

PLA. I would.

SOC. And, again, that those things that never exist may never be known?

PLA. Never.

102 *Release Thyself*

SOC. Then those things that never are also may never be imagined?

PLA. They cannot, as I have said.

SOC. It appears then that my primary division was too simple, and should thus be corrected, into those things that are and those things that sometimes are.

PLA. It is a good correction, Socrates.

SOC. That yet remains to be seen. But concerning those things that are, may they also be divided in a similar manner?

PLA. I imagine that they may.

SOC. Then let us do so – in the first place into those things that sometimes are, and those things that always are.

PLA. As the man who does not assume anything, Socrates, I cannot admit this division.

SOC. Why so, Plato?

PLA. For this reason: that I can readily perceive of many things that sometimes exist and sometimes do not, but where in all of these, and in the whole of the universe, can that which always is be seen?

SOC. Where indeed? And whether we perceive the whole of the universe; but of that we may consider later. Then shall we say that because those things that always are cannot be seen, either by you or others, that they thus have no existence at all?

PLA. I think that we should.

SOC. Then are we to dispense with them, as we have already dispensed with that which never is?

PLA. We are.

SOC. Thus we shall be left with only those things that sometimes are, dismissing as nothing those things that never are and those that always are, as being equally non-existent and redundant of any reality whatsoever.

PLA. That is indeed what we are left with, Socrates.

SOC. Together with, should we not assert, these same things which sometimes are not?

The Platon   103

PLA.   Yes, we should assert this also.

SOC.   In such a manner that the same things both sometimes are and sometimes are not; is this a fair summary for this moment?

PLA.   It is fair.

SOC.   I hardly think so, Plato.

PLA.   Why do you not, Socrates?

SOC.   For this simple reason, my friend: that whatever is not cannot be said *to be* in any manner or form, or would you say otherwise?

PLA.   I would not.

SOC.   Then can it be that something that is not can ever become something that is, whether sometimes or always?

PLA.   (*After a considerable pause*)   I must admit that I do not know or imagine how this could possibly happen.

SOC.   Does it not then follow that whatever becomes something that is not, cannot ever become something that is again?

PLA.   It does indeed appear to follow.

SOC.   Then it seems now to me, my friend, that I was foolish in my attempt to divide the universe in any manner whatsoever. For it now presents itself to be constituted solely from those things that sometimes are. And further, that when these same things pass out of existence, and then are not, that this condition is not a temporary one, but permanent, and that they will never be again, for they have thus become nothing.

PLA.   Indeed, Socrates, the universe does appear to be thus now.

SOC.   And does it also appear, that the difference in the condition of all things that sometimes exist is simply in the extension or brevity of such existence, be it ever so long, or ever so short, or some one of the many measures in between?

PLA.   It does appear so, that this is the condition of all such things as these.

SOC.   But what? If this is indeed the condition of all the things in the universe, will it not also be as such for the universe itself, and this even more so?

PLA.   It is thus inevitably so.

SOC. Then it must follow from this that at some time to come, regardless of its apparent extension, the universe itself will pass out of existence, together with time and matter and whatever else it contains; and this forever and into nothingness. Is this, then, a reasonable prediction?

PLA. It is indeed, according to our present reasoning.

SOC. Then we should look now to the cause of all this, and thus complete the picture.

PLA. I agree that we should at this point, but in what way do you suggest?

SOC. In this way, and we should ask this simple question.

PLA. Only ask the question, Socrates.

SOC. Can we assign a name to that cause which makes something that sometimes is to become nothing and forever?

PLA. We can and do assign a name to that cause, and the name of it is death.

SOC. And is this death, then, the condition of that which sometimes exists ceasing to exist?

PLA. It is so.

SOC. Then again it appears that the universe itself is destined to death and non-existence – or does it appear otherwise to you?

PLA. It does not.

SOC. What then will be left after the death of the universe?

PLA. Nothing at all will remain.

SOC. And must it not happen then, at the extinction of the universe, that it thus will be once and forever?

PLA. It could indeed only happen once, and that forever.

SOC. That is so. We can, then, see plainly to what end the universe and all that it comprehends is moving towards, and this inevitably and inescapably so.

PLA. At this moment we most surely can.

SOC. Yet what can we say of its beginning?

PLA. I am not at all sure what we can say of this.

SOC. Come, dear Plato, you play your part too well. You have affirmed much concerning the end and death of the universe and all that it contains; is there then naught that can be said of its beginning and birth, by the man who still assumes nothing? Or do you say that the universe itself never had any beginning?

PLA. I can only say that it must have had some beginning.

SOC. Why is that so very necessary, dear friend?

PLA. Because the only other standpoint, if in truth this universe exists at all, is that it has always existed; and we have already dismissed all such things that always are.

SOC. We have dismissed them as being invisible. Then do you now say that all things that sometimes are, and indeed the universe itself, not only will end and cease to exist, but that they also had some beginning and a start of such an existence?

PLA. I do.

SOC. What then do you say was the condition prior to this beginning and start?

PLA. It was obviously the condition of nothingness.

SOC. And is this nothingness the same with that to which everything is destined at the end?

PLA. It is.

SOC. In summary then, my friend, all things that sometimes exist arise and have their beginning from nothing, exist for some period of time, and then descend back into this same nothingness, and this only once and forever. Is this an accurate account of your position?

PLA. It is accurate.

SOC. And would you then say that this nothingness is of such a kind as will not admit any addition to it?

PLA. I would and do say so, as otherwise it would it would be something.

SOC. Then of this nothingness itself, do you say that it possesses any energy of its own?

PLA. I do not.

106 *Release Thyself*

SOC. And does it exert any power in addition to its being nothing?

PLA. It does not.

SOC. What, then, of essence? Does nothing have an essence of its own, so as to be something?

PLA. It cannot have any essence, as it is not.

SOC. What then could cause this condition of nothingness to change?

PLA. I do not understand your question.

SOC. Then I will make it clearer for you. What is it within this state of nothingness, which was previous to the beginning and birth of all things, which enables these same things, and the universe itself, to come into existence, even for the most fleeting moment of time?

PLA. There cannot be anything in this nothing that enables these things to begin, as it is truly nothing, completely and utterly.

SOC. And the universe, and all that it can possibly contain, does it have the power to raise itself from nothingness, as existing there potentially but not actually?

PLA. It does not, as it also cannot be there, for there is nothing else there than nothing; and nothing is the potential of nothing.

SOC. How, then, can the universe arise into existence or have a beginning, or become to be at all, when it does not exist in or separate from this state of utter nothingness?

PLA. It cannot.

SOC. Then is it possible that from something that never is, something that sometimes is can arise or become at all?

PLA. I do not see how it can be possible.

SOC. It can only be then, my unassuming friend, that this universe does not exist at all, even for a moment, as there is nothing prior to it, or in it, or after it, that possesses the power to bring it into such existence from nothingness. And this conversation is not happening, nor ever will, as you and I do not exist; nor do those who may hear or read of us; nor any or all animals of every kind; nor elements or planets or suns and stars, or galaxies and cosmoi or time or any and everything else – and even death itself does not exist – for nothing prevails over and is the very all.

The Platon 107

PLA. (*After a considerable pause*) This is a hard, unsatisfying, but necessary conclusion, Socrates, if existence itself is but a temporary condition; and it reveals that very absence of reality which must be the very principle, substance and end of all things.

SOC. It does indeed, in all of its proud and ignorant nakedness. (*He then subsides into silence for a few moments.*) But come, my brave friend, let us examine all of this in another manner.

PLA. What other manner do you suggest?

SOC. If, then, existence is thus, what does it pronounce concerning life?

PLA. I cannot say at this moment.

SOC. Shall we then attempt to divide the universe in a similar manner, such as into things that sometimes live and things that always live?

PLA. We could indeed attempt such a division, but I reason that a similar result would await us. For, again, where do we see that which always lives? And further, if existence itself is either temporary or not at all, neither can there be that existent which is said to live, or to move, or to be moved.

SOC. Then we are saved both time and energy, as the concluding opinion, yet again, can only be that whatever appears to sometimes live does not even live at all, but for a moment, as it is the false motion of a false existent, or can we say other than this?

PLA. We cannot.

SOC. And do you perceive that other and similar conclusions will result for whatever we hold on to as most precious?

PLA. What do you mean by this, Socrates?

SOC. All such things as in general are considered to be true. For if existence and life are not at all, neither will there be anything to know or be known by, or to love, or to believe in, or to aspire to, or that is just, or good, or evil, or beautiful, desirable, or anything else of the kind. For all and everything is untrue, unnecessary and unimaginable, possessing no substance or use or attraction.

PLA. Where, then, can we go from this position, Socrates, which is the result of such a reasoning?

108　*Release Thyself*

SOC. This is not reasoning, O man of the world, but a sophisticated and ignorant opinion dressed as wisdom, born from the most cursory and facile observations.

PLA. But it is an opinion that is and will be held by very many.

SOC. The premise may well be but the conclusion will not, nor the kind of life it would promote; as it sponsors only nothingness and pointlessness, even in the holding of such an opinion, and is like a naked man pretending to be clothed, though his nakedness is obvious to all whose eyes are not closed.

PLA. But again I say, where can we go from here in order to approach the answers to my questions?

SOC. Let us begin again thus, and for this time let us attempt to truly reason and to bring light into this popular gloom. Do you say, then, that we do not see either that which is always or that which lives always?

PLA. I do.

SOC. Then what is it in us that does not see these things?

PLA. I do not understand what you are asking, Socrates.

SOC. Again, dear friend, you play your part full well, as that representative man. But answer to this instead. Do you say that because you do not see anything that always is, that therefore there is no such thing, or merely that you do not see it?

PLA. I say both. As I do not see it because it does not exist, and because it does not exist I cannot see it.

SOC. And yet, I presume, you have looked for these things and, not finding them, you have concluded that they do not exist. Is this then the case with you?

PLA. It is indeed.

SOC. And what were you looking for them with − which power have you employed in this search?

PLA. That power which all men use, my sense of sight and my eyes.

SOC. These eyes then that you use: do you say that they are everlasting?

PLA. Most certainly not.

SOC. Yet do they not see things which existed before they ever saw them, either for a short or for an extended duration?

PLA. Yes, they do.

SOC. And can they see things which have not yet come to pass or into existence, as being of some future period?

PLA. They cannot.

SOC. But can you not perceive of some things yet to come, such as my death, or your own, or even the morrow's sunrise?

PLA. But of course I can, as can all mankind.

SOC. Yet your eyes announce to you that I am here now, but not that I shall not be by tomorrow's end, or what would you say?

PLA. I say that my eyes do indeed inform me that you are present, but my opinion and imagination that you may not be tomorrow.

SOC. And what if I were permitted to leave this cell, would not your eyes then fail to see me?

PLA. They would.

SOC. But from this would you deduce that I did not exist at all?

PLA. I most certainly would not, as my opinion would deduce it to be otherwise.

SOC. Then do we not have more than one way of seeing? For in addition to this sensible sight, have we not discovered imagination and opinion?

PLA. I admit these three, and that we have.

SOC. And which of these would you rely upon for announcing something of the truth?

PLA. It appears to me, Socrates, that each of them in its own way announces some element of the truth.

SOC. Though would you accept the sensible evidence that the flower on yonder table is no bigger than your thumbnail?

PLA. I would not, for I know that it is considerably larger.

SOC. What then, good man, of number, and measure, and of time itself?

110 *Release Thyself*

PLA. What of them, Socrates?

SOC. Could a man, or any other similar animal, not only perceive of these, but compute, comprehend and utilise them, if he did not possess some power that can see and understand wholes and parts and the relationships between them, and their very essence, which is hidden from all sensible and doxastic inspection?

PLA. He could not.

SOC. And would he be able to recognize not only the boundary of the present, but also the infinity of the past and the indefinite extension of the future, if he were not in possession of some power that can grant him this mighty ability?

PLA. Again, Socrates, he would not.

SOC. Then do you not now see that time itself either never was, is, or ever will be, or that it is once and always and of the nature of *only*?

PLA. I do see it as such and very clearly, and that it can only be truly of the latter.

SOC. Now, direct your gaze, Plato, to the cause of time and of all such number and measure. For time itself, being a whole comprehending three parts and many measures, will appear to you to be caused by something that is a whole prior to any parts, and a permanent stable motion that always is the same, and never was nor ever will be different from that which it simply is. And perceive further of this nature that what is present to it is ever present, and that it admits of nothing that was before it or that shall be after it, as it is the bond of all things that can ever be said to truly be, whether always, sometimes, or becoming to be.

PLA. I perceive at present such a nature as this, and declare that I am astonished by such a beautiful vision.

SOC. What, then, do you say that all these powers of seeing and of knowing have in common?

PLA. (*After a pause*) You must answer for me your own question, Socrates, for I am at present at a loss as to what that is.

SOC. Does it not appear to you to be contact? And that without such contact it is not in the least possible for anything to see or to know anything else?

PLA. That is indeed how it appears to me now.

SOC. Then shall we conclude that if a man wishes to see something that always is, he should use that power which is of a similar and kindred nature to its object, and that by this alone will he be able to contact and to know it.

PLA. That is a wise and inescapable conclusion.

SOC. Do you think then, Plato, that a similar reasoning may be applied in your search for that which lives always and that which always lives?

PLA. Indeed I do, Socrates.

SOC. In brief, then, we could reason that there are those things that live for a time, be it ever so long or short, and other things that simply live and to which time does not accede; as they are seen as such natures to which the past and the future cannot be predicated – being ever-present in both their essence and their life.

PLA. We could and should reason in this sublime manner, for now we speak of eternity and of all things eternal.

SOC. It appears that we do indeed, no matter how poorly. But come, let us examine with whatever power we possess what must surely follow from these reasonings. We admit then, that there are those things that live always, and to which no part of time is present, as they never were other nor ever will be other, but simply are always.

PLA. This we do admit.

SOC. And do we not also perceive, according to the common senses and opinion, many and varied things that live only for some part of time, and then are past, and will not be again?

PLA. Yes we do, as do all men.

SOC. What then, Plato? Do not these two conditions appear to you to be as opposite as it is possible to conceive of? I mean, that which is always and lives always, and to which there is neither anything past or yet to come; and that which is sometime and lives sometime, and according to which the past, the present and the future define its temporal existence.

PLA. Yes, Socrates, they do appear to be wholly opposed to each other.

112 *Release Thyself*

SOC. And further, that the one is transcendentally independent of all time, and that the other is completely dependent upon it. Does this appear clearly to you now, my friend?

PLA. It is very clear to me at this time.

SOC. Do we not then, to repeat and bolden, call those things that subsist independently of time eternal?

PLA. We do.

SOC. And those things that are inseparable from time, do we resist from denominating them temporal?

PLA. We do not, as it most plain that their nature is as such.

SOC. This opposition, then, must necessitate at least one other nature in order that communication and contact can exist between these two conditions, which appear to be so mutually exclusive. Or how do you say, Plato?

PLA. It is indeed a necessity.

SOC. What will this be – this nature that exists as a medium for that which is independent of time and that which is time dependent?

PLA. (*pausing*) Surely, Socrates, it is time itself, which enables the one to be present to the other.

SOC. But what then, Plato? Do you say that those natures which are independent of time are themselves indigent of time for some one or other of their activities?

PLA. I see that it cannot be so, for otherwise they would cease to be unindigent of time.

SOC. And in ceasing, which is a cessation of some action, they would then hardly be eternal natures in energy, or do you say otherwise?

PLA. I do not.

SOC. What then follows, dear man? Must it not be one of two things?

PLA. Of what two things do you now speak?

SOC. I speak of these, Plato – that either time itself is temporal, or that it is essentially eternal and extends through power its energies as its parts, and this without inception or cessation.

The Platon 113

PLA. This is a remarkable consideration, Socrates, and I can only think that the truth of it must be of the latter.

SOC. And in such a state, will it be the case that all temporal natures, and that exist for some part of time, will be wholly dependent upon it for such an existence?

PLA. Yes, it does appear to be so at this moment.

SOC. Yet what, Plato, do you say to this, before you so readily agree with such reasoning?

PLA. Say to what, Socrates?

SOC. Surely this, my friend; that those natures which depend upon time, depend upon it for the period and measure of their existence, but not for the existence itself. Or how does it appear to you?

PLA. (*After a long pause*) That indeed must be so, master, for the offspring of time must be times, and not those existences which are measured by them.

SOC. Then have we not arrived at some station in our enquiry?

PLA. We have.

SOC. And is it not one such as this, that those natures which are indigent of time for the extension of their existence, must depend upon something else for the very existence itself?

PLA. Indeed I believe it is.

SOC. And yet time communicates itself to all those things that so depend upon it.

PLA. I cannot doubt that it does.

SOC. And in communicating does it not contact?

PLA. It does.

SOC. And this for every moment of that existence?

PLA. Again, it must be so.

SOC. And in contacting, through every indivisible moment, does it not then know both what it is contacting and what is contacted?

PLA. This remarkable truth must follow.

114 *Release Thyself*

SOC. And do we not denominate, by any other name, that nature which knows, intellectual?

PLA. We do and rightly so.

SOC. Then time itself must be a profoundly intellectual being, existing both in itself and in others, on the one hand eternally and on the other eternally and temporally.

PLA. I cannot admit that it could be otherwise, Socrates.

SOC. I think then, dear Plato, that we are at some mid-point in our enquiry, and should invite new breath before we continue.

PLA. We should, father, as I am certainly in need of it.

SOC. Then we must truly pray that the God who cares for philosophy inspires us.

PLA. That is ever my ardent desire and prayer.

SOC. (*After a pause*) Yet I will go back a little way, Plato, before we again proceed.

PLA. Back to what, Socrates?

SOC. We said, I think, that the apparent opposition between the eternal and the temporal required at least one other nature in order for a continuous communication between them, did we not?

PLA. We did so.

SOC. And we discovered that time itself was a medium between these conditions.

PLA. We did.

SOC. Yet being such a medium, can we then say that it is the cause of their union, in whatever way that may come about, or only that it is an element of such a mixture?

PLA. In some lucid manner, Socrates, I can only see that it is the latter. For if time was the sole cause of the unapparent union of eternal with temporal natures, it would not only dominate the latter, but also the former, which, to me, appears in this light to be impossible.

SOC. The cause of this and other such like unions, must then be something over which all eternal and temporal natures can never exert any power.

PLA. It must be so.

SOC. And can we name so great a principle?

PLA. I cannot, but can only believe that there is such a venerable one.

SOC. Let that, then, be sufficient. (*After a considerable pause*) Are you prepared, my friend, to proceed, after we have shared this water?

PLA. I am, Socrates, and most willingly.

SOC. So come, noble Plato, and let us follow our light. We have already conceived that time is the boundary of temporal existence, but that it is not the cause of the existence itself. Do you recall this?

PLA. I do.

SOC. And do you also remember that we understood there to be eternal existences which are independent of time; temporal existences which are wholly dependent upon time for their duration; and time itself, which appears as an intelligent medium between the two?

PLA. Again, I do so remember.

SOC. What then? Is it that we propose that there are some things that live eternally, and some things that live temporally, yet that there are none that live with and throughout the whole of time and whether in one or all of its total parts?

PLA. It seems, so far, that we do, Socrates.

SOC. Then surely this cannot be, Plato, if our former reasoning was certain. For there are these two things that must be considered.

PLA. What two things do you mean?

SOC. Life, and the extension of life. The former considered as the motion of being, and the latter as its measure.

PLA. This is certain.

SOC. And is it also certain that whatever lives eternally is without the measure of time?

PLA. It is.

SOC. And that whatever lives temporally is bound by the measure of time?

PLA. This also is certain.

116 *Release Thyself*

SOC. What, then, can we say of that which lives throughout the whole of time?

PLA. It can only be that it is of such a medium nature between eternal and temporal life.

SOC. And this in a similar manner to time itself?

PLA. Similar and kindred indeed.

SOC. And time itself, then, being essentially eternal through the *always* it contains, yet energizing according to this *always* through the whole of its parts, is participated by a similar nature which lives consubsistently with it and in a similar manner – is this then what we now reason?

PLA. I own that it cannot be otherwise.

SOC. And do you say that time is many or one?

PLA. I say that it is both.

SOC. Then what do you say of the lives which participate of it; that they are also many and one?

PLA. I do, certainly, according to this reasoning.

SOC. Do you mean by this that there is one time and also many times, dependent upon this one?

PLA. I do.

SOC. And immediately conjoined with these, do we now perceive that there is one life according to the one of time, and many lives according to time's numerous generations?

PLA. I do not see how we can say otherwise.

SOC. We could, Plato, but for the present it is sufficient. Yet, my friend, let us examine this in greater detail in order to come closer to your original question. Let there be two existences, such as two similar bodies; which of these then would be the better?

PLA. How will I make this judgment, Socrates?

SOC. In this manner: do you not say that whatever being always is likewise always lives?

PLA. I do, and most certainly.

SOC. And what of the being that sometimes is: does that not also sometimes live?

PLA. It does.

SOC. Again, then, examine these two bodies, both of which exist for a time. Yet one of them simply exists, while the other exists and is alive. Which of these two is commonly understood to be the better?

PLA. It is certainly the body which is also alive.

SOC. And did we not perceive that whatever lives for sometime, receives this vital power of living from that which lives through the whole of time?

PLA. We did so perceive, and even now I do.

SOC. Then we have these three things before us: the nature which lives through the whole of time, the nature which lives through some part of time, and the nature which is vitalized from these and is alive for a period only, or do we say otherwise?

PLA. We do not, Socrates.

SOC. Yet even now we must also remember that nature which lives independently of time, and upon which time depends for its very existence and life.

PLA. This we must always remember.

SOC. And would it be fair to call this nature life itself, or eternity, or something of the like?

PLA. It would be both fair and beautiful to denominate it so.

SOC. What more could we say of this singular eternity, Plato, and of its relationship with time?

PLA. I imagine that very much more could be said and, according to our present discovery, it should be asserted that eternity or some eternal nature is indeed the very father and generator of time.

SOC. And did it not appear to us that time is a profoundly intellectual being?

PLA. It did, and it still appears to me to be as such.

118   *Release Thyself*

SOC.   But does it appear to you to be possible that any nature can generate anything from itself, if it does not comprehend in itself that which is to be generated?

PLA.   It seems to me that it is impossible that such a thing could ever occur.

SOC.   What, then, if the nature to be generated is of the intellectual kind; must not its generator comprehend it as a truly intellectual conception?

PLA.   It must and very certainly.

SOC.   And this intellectual conception, must it not involve also the very life of that which is to be generated?

PLA.   Again, it surely must.

SOC.   So that it not only simply is, but is fully alive, and glittering with intellectual and generative power.

PLA.   Indeed, Socrates, it appears to be so, and very beautifully.

SOC.   Come, then, and name this being that is a life resplendent with intellectual power, conceived in and by eternity, replete and alive with each and all of its possibilities and generations.

PLA.   (*after a pause*) I do not know its name, Socrates.

SOC.   Nor do I, dear Plato, know this name as conceived by its generator and nurse; but by us it is denominated *idea*.

PLA.   I see now that it is, and that it is in truth a very good and powerful name.

SOC.   Is, then, the idea of something the same as the reason of that same thing, and even the thing itself?

PLA.   (*after another pause*) I must say that it is not. For it appears to me that the idea of something comprehends in itself the reason of that same thing.

SOC.   Yet is it possible, Plato, that anything can exist if there is no reason of that existence?

PLA.   I do not see how that could be possible.

SOC.   And that reason of existence, like the existence itself, is it generated from the idea of all such existences?

PLA. It must be so, Socrates.

SOC. But just a little before, did we not say that idea is full of life and is alive?

PLA. We did.

SOC. Did we not also understand that the existence itself was alive, in a similar manner, for some or all of time?

PLA. Again, we did, Socrates.

SOC. But that it is not possible for a thing to exist if it is truly separated from the reason of such existence, or does not possess a reason in some manner: is this what must follow by necessity do we say?

PLA. We do.

SOC. Then does it also follow that the reason of anything is generated from idea, and is the life of the thing itself and gives to it life?

PLA. This does follow and beautifully.

SOC. But what do you say, Plato? Does not that which comprehends idea also comprehend all the reasons it contains?

PLA. This must indeed be so.

SOC. And in comprehending idea, and all the hidden vital reasons it contains, is it not necessary that it brings these reasons to light, and generates them, and bestows upon them something of itself together with the life which is of their very essence?

PLA. It is not only necessary but truly desirable.

SOC. Come, then, and let us see some of the implications of this evolution.

PLA. There is naught else I would rather see at this moment.

SOC. Hence, then, in the first place, we have two distinct lives and existences, the first being of the nature of eternity and is eternal, comprehending in itself everything that can possibly be generated from it, and which we now call idea. Secondly, we have that life which is temporal and exists for some measured period of time, and is then bound by such a measure. Yet we then discovered another form of life, which though consubsistent with time, is so for the whole of it and its total parts. Is this an accurate summary so far?

120 *Release Thyself*

PLA. It is.

SOC. But does it appear to you probable that the nature which exists for the whole of time will be immediately conjoined with that which has only a fleeting existence, such as body; as if that body was necessary for its perpetual existence, and without which its existence would be incomplete?

PLA. It does not appear at all probable. For that nature which lives through the always of time will be independent, always, of that which exists physically and for but a measured period.

SOC. So that it will be necessary that there should be some other nature, which is always moved by that which lives and moves itself through the always of time, and which in turn moves that which lives for some duration, whether extended or brief, and is for that time moved and has the appearance of life.

PLA. It will be indeed very necessary.

SOC. Then does it not appear that we have these four conditions of life – that which is eternal and is independent of time, and is eternally alive with a stable motion and life about the *same*, and which we name idea; that which lives throughout the whole of time, being dependent in a certain manner upon such wholeness and its total parts, always generating life from itself and moving itself, being the very reason of everything that is moved; and thirdly, that nature which is always moved by the reason of things, as being by a certain essential compulsion, and from which it is generated, and which in its turn, being so moved by its generator, moves all things that have any sort of life that is measured by some part of time and is temporary?

PLA. It does so appear, Socrates, and yet very much is hidden and involved in these briefly stated four conditions.

SOC. That is so. But let us be even more concise, as our time here is short, and denominate them idea; the reason of things (or soul); nature, which cannot but be moved than by its reason; and body, which is alone moved by the nature which is itself moved by its reason or soul. But even now we have come to the heart of your question, Plato, concerning the soul of man, which is the very living reason of man and of all that depends upon it.

PLA. It seems that we have indeed, and already the answer is dawning upon my sight.

SOC. And did it not just now appear to us that all such things that are said to live for a time, are generated by the nature that is moved by its reason or soul?

PLA. It did appear so and very brightly.

SOC. And being always moved by its reason, it is not then the same as that reason or soul.

PLA. It is not the same.

SOC. Yet can it be truly separated from it without perishing?

PLA. It must perish if this were ever possible.

SOC. Then that which is not reason is moved by that which is, would you then say?

PLA. I would and I do.

SOC. Then let us strike the centre, as the saying goes, and dare to affirm that there is one only universe consisting of all things, and that this universe has one reason for being and living, and it will always be the same reason throughout the whole of time, and that this very reason is the very soul of the universe. And further, that this reason or soul generates from itself and from its eternal idea, all the reasons of all things that subsist according to nature; and that all bodies and all physical lives of all animals and natural existences are born from nature through the power of its reason, and can no otherwise exist even for any part of time.

PLA. I cannot but just contemplate such a beautiful order, Socrates.

SOC. But consider this now, Plato. Do you say that there is a reason of man, and then reasons of the multitude of mankind?

PLA. I do.

SOC. And that these very reasons are souls, being the self of each man and the one?

PLA. Again, I do say that this is true.

122 *Release Thyself*

SOC. Then will it not be true also, that because the self of man is the same as its reason, then it can never be separate from itself or truly depart from itself?

PLA. It appears that it will very much be true.

SOC. And would you then agree, that the reason of the universe itself, being generated by that which comprehends its idea and all the ideas of all it contains, in itself comprehends the reason and reasons of man?

PLA. I would agree and readily do so.

SOC. And this together with the reasons of all the other animals and existences it contains?

PLA. Together and wholly, Socrates.

SOC. Then, how do you say; is it possible for anything to know its own reason?

PLA. It must be so if that reason possesses such a power.

SOC. Yet that which is born from non-reason, can that know but through its non-reason?

PLA. It cannot.

SOC. But in as much as they are connected and contact each other, did we not say that this will then be some kind of knowledge?

PLA. We did indeed say as much.

SOC. And in those natures where the reason is the very self, it will be that reason knowing itself and being itself.

PLA. It will be.

SOC. But what of that which is non-reason? Can that nature know that which is reason?

PLA. In as much as there is contact it can, but after the manner of non-reason.

SOC. Then we must now ask this necessary question.

PLA. Do but ask it, Socrates.

SOC. I will and it is this. Does any or every man know himself, that is, his very reason and soul?

PLA. I believe that some men do and have done, but that they may be rarer even than gold.

SOC. What, then, of the bulk of mankind; do they then not know their reason, but from a willing and prolonged sympathy with that which is generated are involved in the vastness of the non-reason suspended from them and upon which their bodies depend for all that they know and enjoy?

PLA. They are.

SOC. And what of other reasons or souls? Do you imagine that some who are wholly divine and angelic, and others of the kind, and even that of the universe itself, will always know themselves, together with their generators and that which they generate?

PLA. I am sure that there must be souls such as these living and whole reasons.

SOC. For it appears that there are no ideas of individuals, but that there are many reasons of such.

PLA. This appears to me to be very clear.

SOC. And others being non-reasons or irrational souls only, who are obedient to the decrees and the governance of reasons, who need not to know themselves, as their happiness and evolving perfection is from their being ever-filled from the powers of reason, and flowing into the infinity of existences in the past and in the future, delighting more in being and living than in knowing – do you perceive that there are many such natures as these?

PLA. I do, and such natural lives are multitudinous and beautifully varied.

SOC. Yet one there is with the capacity to know itself, to know the very reason of its being, but who does not all the time and is thus partial, having the power to verge to its reason, to non-reason, or to ideas and the intellects that comprehend them. For what else can comprehend ideas but mind?

PLA. There is nothing else, Socrates.

SOC. Then in these two lives, Plato, is the necessity of man to be found – either to generate and to be as an irrational animal or as a divine one, to be ruled or to be the ruler, ever the choice of the self-motive reason.

124 *Release Thyself*

PLA. What is it you mean when you say to be the ruler?

SOC. To be ruler and leader of himself and then to be ruler and leader of his kind, together with the generation of the multitude of natural lives that fill this mighty universe. For as wolves are led by wolves, and lions are led by lions, so are sailors led by captains and tribes of souls by souls that know themselves and the reasons of their existence, and the essence and power which generates them, and are their leaders. Hence the purpose of man to the universe is to be and to know his reason and, in doing so, to play his proper part in the generation and conversion of beautiful beings and lives, as do all other natures surrounding him in their own peculiar manner and for good.

PLA. (*after a long pause*) Does this then mean, master, that man needs the universe to know and fulfill his reason, and that the universe needs man for its fulfillment?

SOC. Nay, Plato, say not that the universe needs man for its fulfillment, but that it wants man to be a beautiful life for the benefit of all lives that depend upon him. Yet, if he does not become so, then still the universe will always be happy, apart, that is, from mankind. But that man needs the universe is a truth forever real and beautiful; and in separating himself from it he separates from his cause and thus will perish.

PLA. (*after another pause*) Thank you, dearest Socrates, for this your great assistance.

SOC. Plato, it is only one beginning, the rest is for you to evolve and to discover, for very much was left unsaid and untouched by us.

PLA. I shall never cease in my efforts, master, during this and every life.

SOC. I pray that it will be so, for you are a pupil and philosopher with great merit and potential, who must make his own way very soon, as all of us must at sometime in our brief lives.

PLA. Then I must prepare myself to depart from this baneful place, yet, dear father, my will to do so has fled, and I know not where to find the strength to leave you.

SOC. Then stay, Plato, and await our other friends, who will arrive in but a short time now.

PLA. No, Socrates, I will not stay, though even now my heart strains at the thought of leaving you, and once again it is as if a dark sickness has

The Platon 125

invaded my soul, a dark and angry sickness which will not permit me to speak to any other.

SOC. I know, my dearest son, but it will pass.

(*After a deep and considerable silence, footsteps can be heard approaching the cell door, followed by three gentle taps on it.*)

PLA. (*standing up*) What is this, Socrates, you promised we would be alone?

SOC. Easy, I know not, my friend, as the servant knows well my instructions. Enter!

(*The prison servant enters looking nervous and apologetic, and announces gently to Socrates that he has a visitor.*)

SOC. Tell this visitor, please, to come back here some time later, when my friend and I have finished our time together.

SERV. I will suggest it, master, but this visitor seems intent on being with you now.

(*The servant leaves the cell, and Plato begins to pace the floor, agitated by this unexpected interruption to his final moments with Socrates. Socrates then stands up, yet remains silent with his head bowed. Within a short time the servant reappears.*)

SERV. I am to say to you, master, that the visitor comes to be with both of you, and that, in the name of love, the timing is perfect.

SOC. Then show him in, good man, and bring to us another stool for him to use.

(*The servant leaves the cell.*)

PLA. But Socrates, this is . . .

SOC. Hush, Plato, and anticipate the unexpected!

(*A few moments later the servant returns and puts a stool by the table in the cell. He bows, and departs. A tall hooded figure then enters the cell, clothed in a full-length deep green cloak, and a delightful aroma as of meadow flowers fills the space.*)

SOC. Welcome, visitor, do I know you?

(*Plato advances and is about to speak when the visitor raises a hand as if to silence him.*)

VIS. Yes, Socrates, you know me, as you also know why I am here.

126 *Release Thyself*

SOC. (*Smiling and at the same time bowing his head.*) Diotima! By all the Gods you are now most welcome.

DIO. (*Unveiling her head.*) Dear Socrates, at the last we meet again as you prepare for the next stage of your journey. (*She then embraces Socrates.*)

SOC. That I do, my lady, and in the company of my finest friend and pupil here.

DIO. Plato, I am Diotima, and I know of your love for your master. Will you permit me to share this potent time with you and with good Socrates here?

PLA. (*Bowing his head and descending to one knee*) I know not what to say, Diotima, but that you are welcome, not only by my master but now also by me. In the name of love you are truly welcome, as a light in a place of darkness.

DIO. Raise yourself, Plato, and be at peace for this short time, as we say farewell to our dear friend.

(*Diotima removes her cloak and both Socrates and Plato are astonished at her mature beauty, bearing and dignified aspect. But then she smiles at them, and Socrates laughs, as does Plato, who offers her a stool to rest upon. All three of them sit down.*)

SOC. It is so many years since I have seen you, Diotima, yet those years seem not to have touched you.

DIO. Time touches all of us here, and his marks are made within if not without. But I have seen you many times over these years, and have observed how you progress through life.

SOC. How have you seen me? For I have not seen you since that day upon the mountain, and that night when you revealed to me the mysteries and disciplines of love.

DIO. You have seen me, Socrates, as you have too, Plato, but yet did not know whom you saw, when to that sacred place of celebration you were drawn, and where I appeared to you in unexpected guises.

SOC. (*smiling*) There I perceived much beauty and it surprises me not that you graced those precincts, as even now you grace these with your presence.

DIO. (*also smiling*) Ever you have an eye for the fairness of form, Socrates, and age, I see now, has not dimmed it.

SOC. It has not. For you move me now as ever you did when you found me beginning my quest.

DIO. And your quest has gone well, dear man, as I am sure this young man will testify.

PLA. It has indeed gone well, and innumerable are the benefits which I have received from this excellent man.

SOC. It has been a mutual exchange I can assure you.

DIO. But come, Plato, and share with us your bounty. What do you say is the one benefit you have received which you would place before and above all others?

PLA. (*after a considerable pause*) It is love, Diotima, of wisdom and of truth which has transformed my time on this earth. For without this I know not where I might have turned or what I would then have even become.

DIO. What, then, *have* you become, dear Plato?

PLA. A philosopher, gracious lady, in and from the depth of my soul.

DIO. And if a man or a woman were to enquire of you what that means – to become and to be a philosopher – what answer would you give to them?

PLA. I think that Socrates here is far better qualified to answer this question, and I defer to him in this matter.

SOC. Do not be ungracious or evasive, Plato, for the lady addresses you and for good reason. And I, too, wish to hear what answer you will offer.

PLA. Then my condition now appears to be like this – that what has happened to me has not been by my choice. For who chooses to love anything? Who forces himself into loving? And who falls in love from the dictates of his own or another's will? Not I! For once I had glimpsed the very beauty of truth and the splendour of living wisdom herself, a love burst into my soul like some painless golden arrow, which I could not resist or deny, and which has permeated all my waking moments, together with those in sleep, drawing me and compelling me to pursue with her the very source of this veritable perfect beauty. It overwhelms me. To me, at my age, this is what it means to be a philosopher.

128 *Release Thyself*

DIO. You are in truth your master's pupil in all things pertaining to such love and its ardent ways. This love and its frequent union with its object will be your guide and your guard; and though its way is not easy it is yet simple. But you are not alone in this, for those who love that which is the same will also love each other.

SOC. If, I may say, it is true love.

DIO. You have indeed come of age, dearest Socrates. But what of philosophy herself, Plato?

PLA. What is it that you ask, good lady?

DIO. Only for you to say how she now appears to you.

PLA. She appears to me, then, as a beautiful Goddess and as a sister to that God who is the messenger of and leader to the celestial Olympus. She it is who inspires love into the souls of true philosophers; and she it is who guides such souls to wisdom through herself. She is the lover of lovers and the wisdom of the wise, and to whose beauty my soul is ever drawn.

DIO. And does your love for her extend to actions as well as it does to loving words?

PLA. It does.

DIO. Then you must gird yourself, Plato, with her shield and with her spear, as her way involves war as well as love.

PLA. I do not understand this reference to war, Diotima.

DIO. *Look to your master, philosopher* – is it just love that has brought him to this strait?

PLA. In truth I see that it is not.

DIO. And in war, Plato, virtue then may shine, like never it can in comfort.

PLA. (*looking at Socrates*) Again, I see that clearly now.

DIO. What say you, Socrates, to assist this frightened soul?

SOC. I say that he should listen to you, and learn, and replace fear with wisdom's strength. For philosophy is not immune from the attacks of mighty ignorance, nor yet from those who like to call themselves philosophers.

DIO. What, then, shall I say to this darling pupil of yours?

SOC. Prophesy, priestess! Prophesy, and we will attend to your every word.

DIO. (*after a considerable silence*) Then attend you well to this. Death's cloak will not hide, nor time's swift river obscure, for a light is put before you by your love; and for so long as there are men and women on this earth you will be visible through that light, as will be the light's maker, for by seeing the light you are seen and in being seen the light is yet visible. When this city forgets its mistress then there will not be another, until the great clouds have passed and the cry for her is heard clamouring through all the caverns. All manner of masks men will make to dress up the truth – it is man's way, as in her nakedness they cannot look upon her, for their envy of possession denies her as she is, and dresses her in their own image, hiding her beauty with a face of their own making. When fish, and snakes, and signs and performance attack philosophy's veil, then she will withdraw to whence she came, and the path to her will be forgotten save by those who have heard of the way. Love and wisdom will be separated as the world becomes dry and hard. And then truth will be separated from wisdom as good will be divided from love. Experience will be buried under the giant footprint of experiment, and the men of proud and vain and popular appearance will finally replace lone truth with all the forms of sophistry they can devise, until nothing is left but delightful shells in a dark time. When men forget the Gods they lose themselves, and the children of the wolves ever hasten it in all lands. Dig, and dig deep, until life itself is spent, and tell of her way in secret by shouting, leaving souls to come to tell more – and the more they tell the more secret it will become, for few have the ears to hear her truth when shouting in their very faces. Those who pay great homage to unrolling will not themselves unroll, for men with their feet in the air and their heads in the ground cannot move but in a ludicrous fashion, like freakish plants that can barely germinate, bound for extinction as abhorrent to nature, who will not make things to be upside down. In the name of a school she will be captured, and bound, and stripped and mocked and owned, for so arrogant are the sons of these men. But they will not see that it is not her they have chained for gain, but a lifeless image of themselves, disguised to fool each other, like little children in their parents' clothes all-serious in their pretence of maturity, yet pathetically amusing to adults who can see the imminent dangers and falls of putting on the image of knowledge when the paradigm is unknown. When

130 *Release Thyself*

chance and accident then captivate men's minds because from men's minds were they born, then should the daughters of philosophy take a care for themselves and retire to a beautiful garden and wait for the casualties to find them, asking for remedy and healing – for chance is a man made image of power as accident is of cause. Yet ever these daughters will hasten to their parents as ever the others will not; as a man can see little when his head is in a place it should not be, but for so long as it is comfortable it will yet remain. A frog pretends he is a giant as man pretends that he is wise; but the man knows the frog is not a giant as the God knows the man is hardly wise – for the frog's call is a deceit to others as the man's is a deceit to himself. But that way will yet be plainly secret and cannot be walked but flown. Come, fellow daughters, and fly, raise yourselves beyond all hope of descent or fear of height, as both of them are illusory.

Pass into the spheres of essential life and join with those who are here, and proceed as if in beauty.

Hush! Be silent, now 'tis dark and colour hides with form; there is a presence very near, to each and all – a presence true, and one, full and infinite.

And here above heaven another eye opens, that to see which bounds the hidden vestibule of good's first, purest offspring, in one, infinite and full.

We are not there…

We are not…

We are…

We…

Ssssssshhhhhh…

(*At this point the cell is profoundly silent for many and long moments.*)

DIO. (*standing up*) Socrates, your friends are gathering and await you.

SOC. On which side of the water, dear lady?

DIO. Both here and yonder, good man.

SOC. I am and will remain ready for them.

DIO. And you, Plato? Will you stay here for this time, or shall we depart now and together? My work, like yours, Socrates, is all but done.

The Platon 131

PLA. I will not stay, yet I cannot leave, unless you assist me, Diotima.

DIO. It is for that very reason I came here, Plato. (*pause*) But first I wish to talk with the servant of this place, so I shall leave you to say what you must. (*She then leaves the cell and closes the door.*)

SOC. Well, my fine young man, our time together is all but over for this period; and if you have benefitted to any similar degree as I most surely have from our splendid friendship, then I am happy and content, and thank the Goddess for bringing us together for our mutual aid and succour, and for all of those whom we love and are loved by, be that now or in the unseen future.

PLA. I join with you, dear Socrates, in that prayer of thanks to the saviour. Yet my debt to you seems hardly any less.

SOC. Then if some repayment is due it will be realized by your life. You are an ardent philosopher, Plato, like none I have met before; but you are young, and will be angry for a time – yet turn, and soon, to the sun again, and seek only truth in the universe and in yourself, and penetrate the clouds of opinion with your light, for they cannot ever resist it.

PLA. But even now I know not that which I seek.

SOC. The truth of anything is in its good, my friend; remove that and it will thus cease to be. Opinion cannot but see what it illumines, yet is blinded by such opulent light. When that which is of us is seen as that which is of all, without any exception whatsoever, the sun will then have risen and the source of it made clear. Persist, Plato, with your love of wisdom, and wisdom in her way will yet love you.

PLA. I will, my father, I will, and I shall never let the memory of you grow dim, in me and in this troubled world of men.

SOC. Troubled indeed, Plato, as only man can be, and in this universe naught else is ever lost.

PLA. Yet even now that is what I feel, and will feel it even more when you are gone.

SOC. It will pass for the good, my dearest son.

PLA. I vehemently pray that it will be.

SOC. Then do not pray for what you do not understand, as the Gods know what it is that we love.

132 *Release Thyself*

PLA. Socrates, Socrates, I have one more thing I would ask.

SOC. Only ask it while we still have the time.

PLA. Are you ready, then, to leave this earthly life?

SOC. I have been ready for some long time now, and my feet seem barely to touch the ground. I anticipate a journey to come which I welcome from my very soul. I will be released as I have released and, yes, I am truly ready. Release thyself, Plato, while even yet on this earth, and your soul will be as a magnet for all good men.

PLA. As we speak I know it is happening and I welcome it.

SOC. I hear, my dearest friend, and I am well and deeply pleased.

PLA. Dear, dear Socrates, I know not what else to say.

SOC. Then let our silence be as sufficient as it is good.

(*At this point Socrates embraces the tearful Plato, and then holds his head between his hands and whispers in his ear. Plato looks deeply into Socrates' eyes and nods his head as if in profound agreement, and in turn whispers into his master's ear. They embrace once more. The door opens and Diotima enters the cell.*)

DIO. Are you ready then, Plato, to proceed?

(*Plato then bows to Socrates, whose smile is broad and radiant. He then turns and stands by the cell door. Diotima comes close to Socrates, holds his head in her delicate hands, and whispers gently in his ear, and as he nods she kisses him on his forehead, and then fully on his lips, and then on both his clasped hands. She moves to stand next to Plato, and they both bow low to Socrates, who nods his head and smiles luminously at each of them.*)

SOC. Until another time, my dearest friends.

(*Diotima and Plato then turn and leave the cell together, with an arm held closely around each other's waist.*)

And Socrates engages in deep prayer…

*

* ***** *

Fruits

To Niké

Dear winged Niké, victory divine,
Grant to your suppliants aid and care benign;
Fast at the head of providence you stand
With wings outstretched and triumph in your hand.
Leader of all, who from this mundane sphere
Rise and o'ercome the passions and cold fear;
Maiden of Pallas, with her wisdom crowned,
Of Zeus familiar, protectress profound
Of all heroic souls to good inclined:
By you inspired, benevolent and kind.
And all the Gods proceeding in your train
Defeat dire error, injustice and pain;
Flying before them beauty to uphold,
In war delighting and the spoils of gold,
Which by your arts attract the sons of men,
'Till they regain their natal port again
And cease to war 'gainst that which is their good,
To join with thee in victory's abode
Of peace and calm, once bitter strife is downed,
Replete with harmony and power unbound.
That power from thee which ne'er to weakness tends,
That will to win which nothing earthly bends,
That *providence* which e'er in triumph ends
Pours all around and from it darkness flies -
O stand by me, receive my honest cries
For victory! O Niké hear my prayer
And make my safe return your constant care.

Our Loss

To realize our loss is yonder's gain,
May not bring succour or relief from pain,
When breath itself seems to perpetuate
The shocking gap death wills to generate,
Between the departed and the left behind –
A constant legacy of human kind.
Nor does there ever seem to be a time
When death is welcome as a good sublime;
Too young, too old, too healthy, too infirm,
Too premature to end this earthly term,
Are all the cries throughout our history –
The cries of torment and of misery.
Yet from an overview it can be seen
All that has happened and what might have been,
If all our ardent wishes were fulfilled,
Those of the wise, the clever, and unskilled.
But this the precinct of the Gods remains,
To know what would have been, what earthly gains
And losses benefit the human soul,
What truly tends her nearer to her goal.
And thus the loss of one beloved and true,
The Gods decree, from wisdom's overview,
Is finite, for a time - the loss will end,
And re-united will be friend to friend,
And lover to the loved, in time to see,
That death is granted by divinity
As true re-birth of life and purity,
The path to lasting peace - serenity.

The Voice of Wisdom

I heard the voice of wisdom say,
"My love is calling you;
Wake up, dear soul, from darkness past,
Your life I will renew.
Have faith in me, you will not fail,
Love is the key to all;
With truth's bright ray I will provide,
And with me you ne'er can fall."

I heard the voice of wisdom say,
"The good is all you need;
All else is dreams and phantasy,
Of this you must take heed:
Be prudent of your thoughts and words,
Press to the light within,
To embrace the real with all your heart
And then justice you shall win."

I heard the voice of wisdom say,
"My life is calling you;
It is the very best, dear soul,
All-beautiful and true.
No joy can match this heav'nly peace,
Follow the guide within,
To the meadow and the plain of truth,
Beyond death, and pain and sin.

The Gods are welcoming, have no fear,
Never alone you'll be;
For my path is light and my arms are wide,
Come home, dear soul, to me."

Golden Chain

Let there, however, be one ruler,
One cause of all things, one providence,
And one chain of beings;

Let there be also together with the monad
An appropriate multitude,
Many kings, various causes,
A multiform providence,
And a different order;

Yet every where multitude has
A co-arrangement about the monad,
Things various about that which is simple,
Things multiform about that which is uniform,
And things different about that which is common,
In order that a truly golden chain
May have dominion over all things,
And that all things may be constituted
In a becoming manner.

(Adapted from Proclus' *Commentary on The Timaeus*)

On facing the Morning Sun

O splendid Sun, magnificent and great,
To thee these waking hours I consecrate.
In all the worlds by many names adored,
Light of my life and supermundane lord.
I, in thy radiance bathe, a simple soul
Enwrapt with joy, thy praises to extol
In silent swellings of my inflamed heart,
I contemplate the union you impart;
And stretch to embrace the truth good light contains,
Which leads me back to heaven's pure domains.
Great sovereign Sun! in me your light inspire,
O'erflowing with wisdom and deific fire.

To Mother Earth

Dear Goddess Earth, upon whose ample breast
Terrestrial life depends, please hear this prayer;
And all you other divine elements,
True water, fire, and all-sustaining air:
Unconscious of the need for all you give,
Ungrateful often for your fruits and seeds
And nature's bounty, which in you conceives
That energy by which all things can live.
In all the worlds we find your mighty power,
E'er infinite and wise, and full of life;
Sufficient to unfold the power of heaven,
Of good the first-born and of truth the flower.
We thank you for your gifts, unknown and known,
For your intimate love of all that lives,
For nursing souls with divine strength and care,
For nourishment all-beautiful and fair.
Great Goddess, hear, this hymn of thanks and praise
For all you are and give, for all your ways;
Each living creature owes to you its birth –
All-mighty, life providing, mother Earth.

Life

If all the tools devised were laid before
Men of experiment from now and yore,
And immortality of countless years
Impeded none of them, and held no fears
Of want or pain, or other earthly strife,
And certain time was theirs to spend such life
In measuring and weighing, dissecting,
Or magnifying each and every thing,
And writing formulae of time and space,
Inviting chance to fill the empty place
That all such work discovers at its heart,
Identical to that from which they start;
Investigating what no man will find
Opinion tied and exiled from the mind
Which transcends bodies, nor by them is bound,
Beyond all senses, all such sight and sound,
Whose nature is the only one we see
Available to solve the mystery,
Of what life is and whence it came to be:
Then will we have a world which now we know,
Inflamed by error and with psychic woe.
Let those attempt to measure this in vain,
Though popular, full of material gain;
Such time is short, as is celebrity,
Coursed for oblivion and obscurity –
For life is power, not material force,
The motion of essence is its single source;
And essence itself, replete with power, we see
Is mixed from bound and true infinity,
From that unknown, the one, or unity.
By this alone can essence be revealed,
And life itself will ever stay concealed
From those whose eyes are by the senses bound
In matter's sea and by opinion drowned.
For mind is the eye, and that essentially,
The sight of life and of eternity,
Transcending individuality:
By this we rise, by this we make our flight
Through life's deep heaven, full of beauty, light.

The Heart of Love

From the heart of love shines all-perfect light,
Guiding all who seek beauty unconfin'd,
Bathing life in splendour rich and timeless,
Helping every loving soul regain her sight.

To the heart of love - yes, the path is long,
Hard for those whose hearts fear what is unreal,
Steeper than the sheerest mountain's incline,
Yet upon this path each soul is made full strong.

Round the heart of love choirs of Goddesses
Ever dance and sing, facing the most high,
Bearing souls whose love of divine beauty,
Flies them swiftly to the splendid realms of bliss.

To Beauty

No word, or sound, or mystic pose,
Nor image fair though we compose
The form from forms e'en more sublime,
And work with art through endless time,
Could of this mighty splendour say
The smallest thing about its way.
For soul astonished, quickened and faint,
Relieves herself from all constraint,
Full-fired by love's uprising heat
She strives to see the splendour's seat:
  Beauty, beauty, beauty proceeding,
To the good eternally leading;
Lovely as the source of love,
Symmetry of all above,
Delicate beyond compare,
Splendid beauty every where.
Nectar of Gods, of angels and of men,
This soul is open for your form to illumine;
Be she filled with all virtue, and heaven's sacred fire,
Singing with her god the ancient praises of their sire.
Beyond another, beyond reproach, perfection's dazzling light;
Beyond the stars, both high and low, beyond the realms of night;
Beauty untold! Astonishing my eye,
In silence are you honoured, in wonder do I sigh.

Upon reading Sacred Works

I invoke aid from the heroic race,
All daemons good, and pure angelic grace:
Be with me as these holy words I read,
Quicken in me the intellectual seed,
That from all phantasy I may be freed.
And you, the Goddesses of wisdom's line,
To this thy worst of offsprings, please incline.
Let truth alone be now my living light,
And love direct me through the realms of night,
And faith, to Good, connect me in my flight: for
The Gods are ever present in true prayer,
And shine through words of truth with visions fair;
My soul, for thee, I by this act prepare.

To Socrates

A sage, a saint, a hero born
Bearing light from heaven's morn,
Socrates, friend of Gods and men,
Beauteous soul of happy mien!
May your zeal in wisdom's choir
Enthuse mankind with pure desire,
For every good and truth divine,
Which in your heart doth warmly shine.
No other son of Olympian fire,
Who fast from ignorance doth retire,
Being scorned and celled by impious strife
Could give up more than present life;
But knowing more than mortal kind
That life was given, true life to find,
And by this act the world inspire
To drop attachment and blind desire,
And all conceit sprung from earth-born mind
Through which men blind ever lead the blind.
Philosopher pure in the circle most bright,
Virtuous soul bathed in intellect's light,
Hear me, and hearing, the right hand extend
To this lover of wisdom, a guest and a friend;
And help me to rise from delusion's fierce hold,
To join, with my leaders, that chain of pure gold.

Children of the Sea

Over the river of souls descending
The mother of nature sighs.
Down toward generation's sea
She casts her love-filled eyes.

Her darling children, by currents borne,
To Hades' farthest shores,
Forgetting all while drinking much,
They firmly close their doors.

"My children dear, my children hear,
Unlock your hearts to me;
Though you have moved and turned away,
Lift up your eyes, and see."

But faint the voice falls on the mist
When evening draws her veil,
And deaf they travel ever on
As in their barques they sail.

From within the mother whispers
In each sleeper's ear,
"O watch for me, O look for me,
Be sure that I am near.
Within each breath I lock my power
And give you of my heart;
I am that life that quickens all
By love's all-reaching dart."

To Plato

The heroes' fire for Plato burns full bright,
A master winging from the realms of light;
Whose works and days not even time can hide
From souls of men and generation's tide –
For ever flowing upon some new shore,
To quicken mind's super-abundant store
Of germ like forms, just waiting to receive
That vital light, whereby all things conceive,
And burst full forth with energy divine
Which nothing earthly ever can confine –
A leader, thou, in sun's perpetual train,
To wisdom, good and beauty's fair domain.
No man or woman who to wisdom's seat
Aspires, and turns your page with love replete,
Can fail to recognize deific fire,
If they persist, refusing e'er to tire,
Or turn aside from the inspiring words
Of yours, and those who are the faithful guards
Of knowledge, key to freedom for all men,
Whereby, to heav'n they shall return again,
With eyes wide open and with perfect wings,
To join the choir of demigods that sings
The song of wisdom, which in you doth sound,
Ancient, eternal, full of truth profound.
O Plato, friend to every true divine
And seeker, who the mount of good doth climb,
This thanks and praise from me can ne'er repay
For light received upon the constant way:
Commune with me, both you and all your kind,
Champions perfected by eternal mind;
Commune with me, for my soul yearns to see
The splendours of the father's mystery;
And in this life may I your side attain,
And friendship with the Gods, true bliss to gain.

The Prometheus Trust

www.prometheustrust.co.uk

The Prometheus Trust exists to encourage, promote and assist the flowering of philosophy as the living love of wisdom; and is dedicated to the re-establishment of philosophy as the primary education of the human soul.

The Trust has an extensive and on-going publishing programme, at the heart of which is its Thomas Taylor Series: for details of our catalogue see overleaf.

Our education programme is based on the truth that philosophy is the *love of wisdom*: we welcome enquiries from any individual who is drawn to this affirmation, whether they be well established in the cultivation of philosophy or not. Our website is regularly updated with current details of our courses, as well as one-off workshops and public lectures.

The Trust has been running annual conferences in the UK since 2006 and is delighted by the wide range of participants and presenters, bringing together as they do highly regarded academics together with non-academics – the common ground being a determination to pursue philosophy as a guide to life. The Conference is usually planned for June or July, with its theme and call for papers issued in January – our website carries full details.

Also to be found on the website is our occasional web-journal, *The Meadow*, as well as recent news, several PDF files of interesting texts, and a page of inspiring thoughts drawn from the Platonic tradition, and much more besides.

The Prometheus Trust Catalogue

The Thomas Taylor Series

1 Proclus' Elements of Theology
Proclus' Elements of Theology - 211 propositions which frame the metaphysics of the Late Athenian Academy. 978-1898910-008

2 Select Works of Porphyry
Abstinence from Animal Food; Auxiliaries to the Perception of Intelligibles; Concerning Homer's Cave of the Nymphs; Taylor on the Wanderings of Ulysses. 978-1898910-015

3 Collected Writings of Plotinus
Twenty-seven treatises being all the writings of Plotinus translated by Taylor. 978-1898910-022

4 Writings on the Gods & the World
Sallust On the Gods & the World; Sentences of Demophilus; Ocellus on the Nature of the Universe; Taurus and Proclus on the Eternity of the World; Maternus on the Thema Mundi; The Emperor Julian's Orations to the Mother of Gods and to the Sovereign Sun; Synesius on Providence; Taylor's essays on the Mythology and the Theology of the Greeks. 978-1898910-039

5 Hymns and Initiations
The Hymns of Orpheus together with all the published hymns translated or written by Taylor; Taylor's 1824 essay on Orpheus (together with the 1787 version). 978-1898910-046

6 Dissertations of Maximus Tyrius
Forty-one treatises from the middle Platonist, and an essay from Taylor, The Triumph of the Wise Man over Fortune. 978-1898910-053

7 Oracles and Mysteries
A Collection of Chaldean Oracles; Essays on the Eleusinian and Bacchic Mysteries; The History of the Restoration of the Platonic Theology; On the Immortality of the Soul. 978-1898910-060

8 The Theology of Plato
The six books of Proclus on the Theology of Plato; to which is added a further book (by Taylor), replacing the original seventh book by Proclus, now lost. Extensive introduction and notes are also added. 978-1898910-077

9 Works of Plato I
Taylor's General Introduction, Life of Plato, First Alcibiades (with much of Proclus' Commentary), Republic (& extracts of Proclus' Scholia). 978-1898910-084

10 Works of Plato II
Laws, Epinomis, Timæus (with notes from Proclus' Commentary), Critias. 978-1898910-091

11 Works of Plato III

Parmenides (with a large part of Proclus' Commentary), Sophista, Phædrus (with notes from Hermias' Commentary), Greater Hippias, Banquet. 978-1898910-107

12 Works of Plato IV

Theætetus, Politicus, Minos, Apology of Socrates, Crito, Phædo (with notes from the Commentaries of Damascius and Olympiodorus), Gorgias (with notes from the Commentary of Olympiodorus), Philebus (with notes from the Commentary of Olympiodorus), Second Alcibiades. 978-1898910-114

13 Works of Plato V

Euthyphro, Meno, Protagoras, Theages, Laches, Lysis, Charmides, Lesser Hippias, Euthydemus, Hipparchus, Rivals, Menexenus, Clitopho, Io, Cratylus (together with virtually the whole of Proclus' Scholia), Epistles. An index to the extensive notes Taylor added to his five volumes of Plato. 978-1898910-121

14 Apuleius' Golden Ass & Other Philosophical Writings

The Golden Ass (or Metamorphosis); On the Dæmon of Socrates; On the Philosophy of Plato. 978-1898910-138

15 & 16 Proclus' Commentary on the Timæus of Plato

The Five Books of this Commentary in two volumes, with additional notes and short index. 978-1898910-145 and 978-1898910-152

17 Iamblichus on the Mysteries and Life of Pythagoras

Iamblichus On the Mysteries of the Egyptians, Chaldeans & Assyrians; Iamblichus' Life of Pythagoras; Fragments of the Ethical Writings of Pythagoreans; Political Fragments of Archytas, Charondas and other Pythagoreans. 978-1898910-169

18 Essays and Fragments of Proclus

Providence, Fate and That Which is Within our Power; Ten Doubts concerning Providence; The Subsistence of Evil; The Life of Proclus; Fragments of Proclus' Writings. 978-1898910-176

19 The Works of Aristotle I

The Physics, together with much of Simplicius' Commentary. A Glossary of Greek terms used by Aristotle. 978-1898910-183

20 The Works of Aristotle II

The Organon: The Categories, On Interpretation, The Prior Analytics; The Posterior Analytics, The Topics, The Sophistical Elenchus; with extensive notes from the commentaries of Porphyry, Simplicius & Ammonius. 978-1898910-190

21 The Works of Aristotle III

Great Ethics, Eudemian Ethics; Politics; Economics. 978-1898910-206

22 The Works of Aristotle IV

Rhetorics; Nicomachean Ethics; Poetics. 978-1898910-213

23 The Works of Aristotle V

The Metaphysics with notes from the Commentaries of Alexander Aphrodisiensis and Syrianus; Against the Dogmas of Xenophanes, Zeno and Gorgias; Mechanical Problems; On the World; On Virtues and Vices; On Audibles. 978-1898910-220

24 The Works of Aristotle VI

On the Soul (with much of the Commentary of Simplicius); On Sense and Sensibles; On Memory and Reminiscence; On Sleep and Wakefulness; On Dreams; On Divination by Sleep; On the Common Motions of Animals; On the Generation of Animals; On Length and Shortness of Life; On Youth and Old Age, Life and Death; On Respiration. 978-1898910-237

25 The Works of Aristotle VII

On the Heavens (with much of the Commentary of Simplicius); On Generation and Corruption; On Meteors (with much of the Commentary of Olympiodorus). 978-1898910-244

26 The Works of Aristotle VIII

History of Animals, & the Treatise on Physiognomy. 978-1898910-251

27 The Works of Aristotle IX

The Parts of Animals; The Progressive Motions of Animals, The Problems; On Indivisible Lines. 978-1898910-268

28 The Philosophy of Aristotle

Taylor's four part dissertation on the philosophy of Aristotle which outlines his primary teachings, the harmony of Plato and Aristotle, and modern misunderstandings of Aristotle. 978-1898910-275

29 Proclus' Commentary on Euclid

Proclus' Commentary on the First Book of Euclid's Elements; Taylor's four part Dissertation on the Platonic Doctrine of Ideas, on Demonstrative Syllogism, On the Nature of the Soul, and on the True End of Geometry. 978-1898910-282

30 The Theoretical Arithmetic of the Pythagoreans

The Theoretic Arithmetic of the Pythagoreans, Medicina Mentis, Nullities & Diverging Series, The Elements of a New Arithmetic Notation, Elements of True Arithmetic of Infinities. 978-1898910-299

31 & 32 Pausanias' Guide to Greece

Pausanias' Guide to Greece (in two volumes) with illustrations and extensive notes on mythology. 978-1898910-305 & 978-1898910-312

33 Against the Christians and Other Writings

The Arguments of Julian Against the Christians; Celsus, Porphyry and Julian Against the Christians; Writings of Thomas Taylor from his Collectanea, his Miscellanies in Prose and Verse, and his short works On Critics, An Answer to Dr Gillies, A Vindication of the Rights of Brutes, and his articles from the Classical Journal. Included is a Thomas Taylor bibliography. 978-1898910-329

Platonic Texts and Translations Series

The Platonic Texts and Translation Series presents a number of works from the Platonic tradition in parallel Greek and English, as published by scholars over the last fifty years.

Iamblichi Chalcidensis in Platonis Dialogos Commentariorum Fragmenta
John M Dillon   978-1898910 459

The Greek Commentaries on Plato's Phaedo (I – Olympiodorus)
L G Westerink   978-1898910-466

The Greek Commentaries on Plato's Phaedo (II – Damascius)
L G Westerink   978-1898910-473

Damascius, Lectures on the Philebus
L G Westerink   978-1898910-480

The Anonymous Prolegomena to Platonic Philosophy
L G Westerink   978-1898910-510

Proclus Commentary on the First Alcibiades
Text L G Westerink Trans. W O'Neill   978-1898910-497

The Fragments of Numenius of Apamea (In Preparation)
R Petty   978-1898910-527

Students' Edition Paperbacks

Our Students' Editions are designed to present elements of Platonic philosophy in an accessible form. Some of these paperbacks offer a single dialogue with some modern explanatory essays together with extracts from ancient commentators; others take particular subjects and explore some initial

The Symposium of Plato   Trans. Floyer Sydenham & Thomas Taylor.
Includes Plotinus' On Love (En III, 5), and introductory essays.
978-1898910-978

Know Thyself – The First Alcibiades & Commentary
Trans. Floyer Sydenham & Thomas Taylor. With introductory essays.
978-1898910-961

Beyond the Shadows - The Metaphysics of the Platonic Tradition
Guy Wyndham-Jones and Tim Addey   978-1898910-954

The Unfolding Wings - The Way of Perfection in the Platonic Tradition
Tim Addey   978-1898910-947

The Sophist
With extensive notes and explanatory essays   978-1898910-930

Other titles available from the Prometheus Trust

Philosophy as a Rite of Rebirth – From Ancient Egypt to Neoplatonism
Algis Uždavinys   978-1898910-350

The Philosophy of Proclus – the Final Phase of Ancient Thought
L J Rosán   978-1898910-442

The Seven Myths of the Soul
Tim Addey   978-1898910-374

An Index to Plato A Subject Index using Stephanus pagination 978-1898910-343